Families Can Be Happy

Betty Jane Grams

RadiantBOOKS

Gospel Publishing House/Springfield, Mo 65802

02-0759

DEDICATION

To Monroe,
   Without whose gentle ways in our marriage,
this book could not have been born.

To Mona Ré, Rocky Vaughn, and Rachel Jo,
   Without whom we wouldn't have known if
our parenting really worked.

Library of Congress Catalog Card Number 81-82420
International Standard Book Number 0-88243-759-3
Printed in the United States of America

Contents

Introduction

It was 1968 when God alerted me to the possibilities of sharing with other women through a writing ministry. I had come from the high Andes Mountains of Bolivia, leaving a heavy schedule of ministry in teaching, directing choirs, and running a mission home. I landed in Lima, Peru, a sea-level city, to speak for a women's conference. There, at the Wycliffe missionary rest home, I was isolated in an antiseptic little room. It was furnished simply, with a cot, a chair, and a small table.

My husband was holding a seminar 2,000 miles away in Central America, so I felt very far from him, and quite alone. Before the meeting started, I explored my spartan surroundings. Near a small chapel on the second floor, I found what passed for a library. Three sections of shelves offered outdated *Reader's Digests*, but they still made good reading in that remote area. There were also *The Bobbsey Twins*, some *National Geographics*, and a shelf of new books.

I found women's books and family books. They were all brand new. After checking out several, I took them to my little room. As I read, the walls seemed to recede, and I found myself intently sharing the experiences of other women's lives. Here were contemporary discussions of problems I had personally seen, shared, and lived through!

It was as if a whole new world opened up to me. There, in that remote place, I began to feel that I too should write and share personal and family feelings, family experiences, and maybe even some family secrets.

You may have studied my book *Women of Grace,* which I felt was born out of God's heart especially for us as women. It helped us to look inside and see, "Who am I?" "What kind of woman am I?" "What is my attitude?" "Am I growing spiritually?"

Since that conference in Peru, a growing number of women have asked me to share some of my own experiences and observations for the purpose of strengthening marriage and family life today.

So, with the encouragement of women asking for help, and the nudge of the Holy Spirit, I share with you from God's Word and from my own experiences as a wife and mother.

This book doesn't pretend to offer a comprehensive treatment of any subject, but rather to show from the Word how we can accept and improve some of our closest family relationships.

1

Marriage Is God's Idea

"Our marriage was made in heaven," declared a friend.

My husband answered, "Really? We're working on ours right here on earth!"

Sometimes we quote this to each other, and laugh as it relieves our tensions. We realize that to make a marriage work, we have to work on it.

Marriage is God's idea. Marriage was actually the first institution. It came into being before the Law, before government, and before sin. Here's where reading the Bible helps us to understand the background of marriage.

In the beginning, when God looked at His creation, He pronounced it "good." The earth, the planets, the trees, the light, the fish, the flowers, the animals—all were perfect. He made man to be His companion, but as they walked and talked in the Garden in the cool of the day, He saw that man was lonely. All the animals had companions. He had created them male and female. "But for Adam there was not found a help meet for him" (Genesis 2:20).

So God said, "I will make him a help meet for him" (Genesis 2:18). To provide the helpmeet (or helpmate), God performed the first surgery and formed the woman from the man. She was not from the dust of the ground, but one step more refined. Woman was created from out of the side of man.

A Helpmeet

I love the detail in Genesis 2:21, 22. It says that God put Adam to sleep. In other words, He used some form of anesthesia to perform the first surgical operation. Upon opening Adam's side, He took out a rib and from it formed man's special companion. Having come out of man's side, she is to be loved and protected. She is to walk alongside, to be of equal worth, and to have communion and communication with man. She wasn't made from a bone of the foot to be trampled on, nor from the head to nag and govern him, but from a rib in his side. She was formed out of that which contributes shape and form to the body. So, the woman in turn gives structure and form to the family. She came from a place near his heart—a symbol of her ability to feel and understand the needs of her man.

Can you imagine the reaction of Adam, the once lonely man, when he awakened and God brought her to him. In wonder, Adam said, "This is now bone of my bones, and flesh of my flesh." To all the other creatures he had given names, but with this unique creature, he wanted to share his own name. "She shall be called Woman."

God instituted marriage as a lifelong commitment, but too often in our society it has joined the list of disposables. Still, many marriages endure. Within a single month we received announcements from our friends that four couples were celebrating their 25th wedding anniversary.

To remain married for 25 years is a modern miracle to many people. It is worth working toward.

Marriage is an art—it takes a lifetime of practicing and working together to make the finished product. In fact, we never graduate. Marriage is "till death us do part."

Marriage has many adversaries—social, economic, and spiritual. It is both a demanding and a rewarding commitment. Our spiritual enemy knows that if he can weaken the commitment in marriage and the home, he will strike a blow to the church and weaken the fabric of our nation. His work is insidious.

Fantasy World

One of the main reasons some marriages do not last is that the partners don't take time to think through the strong commitment that marriage requires. They look at the diamonds sparkling in the jewelry store windows, and dream of shimmering wedding gowns. They join in the excitement of their friends' upcoming weddings, and they get carried away with bridal showers and all the fun of the preparations. Entranced by the romantic strains of wedding music, they may scarcely *hear* the serious charge which the marriage ceremony contains.

Our hearts are full of nostalgia at weddings. The flowers, corsages, tuxedos, guest book, cake, napkins with gold initials entwined and a date underneath—all add to the excitement.

We watch while the ushers light the tall white tapers, and pull the white runner down the aisle. The young men look so handsome in their rented tuxedos, so virile, so perfectly groomed. The minister takes his place under the floral arch. The groom is finding it hard to be calm. Here come the girls in their matching lacy, pastel dresses, all so beautiful. Each is carrying a basket of flowers, a single rose, or possibly a lovely painted fan.

The organ swings into a more joyous, more triumphant cadence, "Here Comes the Bride," and suddenly she appears!

Her eyes are sparkling; her feet are light. Her father looks serious, yet excited. He's giving her away. What does that mean? "Who gives this woman to be married to this man?" It seems I hear a tremor in the father's voice when he responds, "Her mother and I." Is he thinking about the day some 20 years before, when he stood waiting for his own bride to float into his life? Or is he thinking how quickly his baby girl has grown into this lovely young woman? Is he remembering how she used to get her days and nights mixed up, or when she had the measles; the times he took her to the dentist, or when he bought her ice-cream cones?

We watch as they stand before the minister. Two tender, beautiful young people, who are worthy to wear the white of virginity with dignity. They've based their lives on the Word of God. The mother dabs her eyes with a lace handkerchief as we listen to the music. . . .

We listen, but do we *hear*? They say, "I do," but do *they* hear the vows?

> "For better, for worse. . .
> For richer, for poorer. . .
> In sickness and in health. . .
> Forsaking all others. . .
> Till death do us part."

They're kneeling and someone is singing:

9

The Lord bless you and keep you.
The Lord lift up His countenance upon you,
And give you peace, and give you peace.
The Lord make His face to shine upon you,
And be gracious unto you. Amen.

Just Beginning

Someone whispers, "It's all over!" Oh, no! It's just beginning. Have they taken time to ask each other questions, or are they afraid of the answers? Have they taken time to talk as well as to touch? What are their goals and objectives? What training, background, and values have molded each of their lives? Do they really mean "in sickness"? What if there is illness or surgery? When pregnancy comes, will the girls at the office seem too attractive to him? Will a night out with the young men eventually be more important than caring for his wife?

Successful Marriage

Marriage is God's idea (Genesis 2:18-25). He instituted it to provide companionship and to complement man (v. 18). For Adam, Eve brought fulfillment; she came to him as a helpmeet. Genesis 2:24 points out that in marriage two become one flesh. Marriage is more than a partnership; it is a miracle of fusion in spirit and flesh of the two partners. They are no longer two, but one.

In Genesis 2:24 we have God's plan as the basis for marriage. Jesus reiterated this in the New Testament: "For this cause shall a man *leave* father and mother, and shall *cleave* to his wife: and they twain shall be *one flesh*" (Matthew 19:5). Here we have three facets of marriage.

1. *To leave*—This is the public, legal decision to leave our childhood home; to make our decision public with a wedding. Now our loyalty must be more toward our mate than to our parents.

2. *To cleave*—This means to be welded, glued to each other, to stick together, to be loyal, to put the other first.

3. *To be one flesh*—This is the physical union.

Marriage not only is a spiritual state, but also must have a physical sexual union. Genesis 2:25 says Adam and Eve were both naked, but not ashamed. Good marriages bring openness in all aspects. We can be ourselves. We can know each other in our hopes, desires, weaknesses, and hurts. We can be open. We don't need to have a veil. Marital intimacy is God's idea. We are created to fulfill His plan.

Jesus started His miracles at a wedding feast. He put His approbation on a wedding. He knew it was a family time and an important celebration for the community. My mother used to say, "When you feel it's time to be married, come home, and we'll have a wedding."

The physical union needs to have the blessing of the marriage sacrament on it. The casual life-style of "just living together" is an experiment in failure. God's way is to leave, to cleave, and to become one flesh. In his book, *I Married You* (New York: Harper & Row Publishers, Inc., 1971), Walter Trobisch likens these three facets to the sides of a tent covering us. When one facet is missing, it's no longer a tent, and then there is no covering.

Unfortunately, the prevalent attitude in schools and literature today often is that marriage is outdated and it makes a woman a slave. This philosophy is propagated openly in many secular colleges. Obviously, we need to know what God's basis for true Christian marriage is.

$$1 + 1 = 1$$

There is a mystical aura about a wedding. We marry through a veil, but when the veil is removed we are faced with reality. There must be openness and communication in order to fulfill the symbolism often expressed in the ceremony. Frequently the two young people will take a candle and light a third candle together. This pictures the fusion of two people into one heart, one life, one flesh, and one home.

The Whole Is Greater Than the Sum of Its Parts

True marriage is more than a romantic attachment, more than butterflies, and even more than a physical union. There must be a uniting of body, intellect, understanding, and spirit. God uses the figure of Jesus loving the Church and giving himself for it. A man is likewise to love his wife with consideration and tenderness. Jesus' claim to authority was in becoming a servant and serving His church. Today the world calls for sexual gratification, with or without commitment. Many do not want to give themselves to be fused into this new mystery, but it is still God's way.

Monroe and I have been married for over 30 years and we still like each other. We enjoy being together. We like to share ideas. We enjoy touching each other. For many years, we have taught courtship, marriage, and family life seminars in

12

many areas of Latin America. A young man named Daniel, who had attended our seminars, said, "We learned more by watching your example of caring, sharing, and loving, than we learned from all the classes, the notes, and the textbooks."

Marriage must be lived! It's God's plan, and it's worth it!

Sharing Time

1. Read the Scripture passages quoted in chapter 1 from various versions of the Bible.

2. Find out which wedding ceremony your minister uses, and read it together.

3. Can you still say, "I do," to each part of it?

4. If not, try to analyze what may have happened in your relationship. How can you work to improve it?

5. Make a list on a sheet of paper with this heading: "Things I Really Like About My Mate."

6. Take a memory trip back to your wedding day. What were some of your ideals and expectations of romance?

7. In what ways has reality been different from the pictures you had hoped for?

8. Express some of these things in dialogue with your mate. Possibly just a time of remembering and sharing would be good for both of you.

9. Perhaps you are not living with a mate for various reasons or circumstances. How can you help someone else who doesn't appreciate her partner?

10. Can you share advice for a meaningful relationship?

11. How can you be a complete person as a single?

2

Commitment Is the Cornerstone

We repeat after the minister in the wedding ceremony, "Thereto I plight thee my troth." The dictionary says this means "to pledge faithfulness, fidelity, loyalty; to give truth or verity, one's word or promise, especially in engaging oneself to marry." Then in parentheses it adds "archaic."

Not only is the expression archaic to some people, but also the idea of fidelity, commitment, and loyalty in marriage is often looked upon as archaic. Many young people enter marriage with the idea, "If it doesn't work, I can get out."

Whenever we undertake anything with a lack of faith, the negative suggestions and influences will win. If we always have an alternative plan, we'll probably use it. But if we are convinced when we set our wedding date, "This is God's will," we will commit ourselves to making it work. God will reveal His will to both parties in a Christian marriage, and He'll help us to fulfill our pledge.

God doesn't do anything in a hurry, and if someone is in a big hurry to get married, watch out. There's probably a doubt somewhere. Felicia said to us, "I know that if I marry Juan, then he'll come to church with me." But marriage is not a fishhook. It took only about 3 weeks after the big church wedding for Felicia to realize this. Not only did Juan refuse to attend church, but he wouldn't allow Felicia to attend either. They were both lost. We must know God's will and realize that marriage doesn't reform anyone. In fact, it accentuates each individual's idiosyncrasies.

More books and magazine articles are being written today on marriage and the family than ever before. And yet, there are also more divorces, more estrangements, more broken homes, and more family problems than ever before. It is the spirit of the age. "In the last days perilous times shall come. For men shall be lovers of their own selves . . . heady, high-minded" (2 Timothy 3:1-4). These are traits that can be present in our personalities, making it difficult to weld ourselves together in a loyal marriage. We find we can't give in. We want our own way. We are egocentric. God help us!

It Couldn't Happen to Me

The attractive face of a well-known woman was featured on the cover of a Christian women's magazine in the fall of 1979. Inside we read the article about the woman and her family, and we were glad to know there still were outstanding people with strong marriages. But a year later that marriage ended in divorce, and problems that had been hidden came to light.

A famous columnist who has given counsel in the newspapers for years always projected a good marriage. Suddenly, after 36 years of marriage, her husband asked for a divorce. She said it was the "gray flannel itch," and that he'd found a woman 29

15

years old, just half of his own 58 years. Therefore, he wanted out of his present marriage vows.

Unfortunately, many marriages are being eroded, and many children are being affected. The National Center for Health Statistics in Washington, D.C. says that for every two couples marrying, one couple is getting a divorce. There were 1.2 million divorces during the year ending in February 1980. Think of the number of people who are suffering hurts, depression, guilt, and anxiety!

Newsweek magazine carried a comprehensive article on "The Children of Divorce." Very often the children of divorce feel it was their fault. I heard some girls sharing about their parents' divorces. One said she was 13 when her parents divorced. She didn't know how to handle it. Her friends ostracized her, and her grades went down. Now, at age 17, she is finally beginning to cope. Another girl said her parents went through divorce proceedings for 5 years, until finally it became "our divorce" for the whole family. Each of the four girls in that family was put into a different foster home. One married early to retaliate, had a baby, and is now divorced. The youngest sister had a baby out of wedlock at the age of 12.

Many girls repeat the errors of their parents, because their mistakes are part of a learned behavioral pattern. Divorce is a deep human hurt. It splits each member of the family right down the middle. It can be more traumatic than death, because divorce is never over.

My friend Robin said he had six or eight parents. He didn't know exactly how many. He had been shunted from one home to another with each divorce and remarriage. Finally, he was reduced to a

16

bewildered, hurt, low achiever. One day, he found a stolen Bible on a shelf in his uncle's library. Since no one really cared where he was, they didn't hunt for him. He began to read, and as he read he found his life and needs pictured. He fell to his knees, and asked that if there was a God, He would reveal himself to him. Robin poured out his hurts to God, and Jesus reached His hand into Robin's torn-up life and healed him. Jesus can undo the tangles of every life.

Submit One to Another

I was in a Sunday school class where they were talking about Christian marriage. They started with Ephesians 5:22 which says, "Wives, submit yourselves unto your own husbands. . . ." Then they went to verse 25, "Husbands, love your wives. . . ." But they overlooked the whole context. Verse 21 says: "Submitting yourselves one to another in the fear of God." Submission is a two-way street. It's not 50-50, it's giving in 100 percent—sometimes one way, and sometimes the other. Refusal to give in is a real problem in many marriages today.

I was listening to an interview with the wife of a prominent personality. She had been his business manager. They were having marital problems and were ready for a divorce. Then a friend testified to her, and Jesus came into her life. After she received the baptism in the Holy Spirit, she was so transformed that all she wanted to do was to talk with her husband about it. Friends had counseled her not to leave religious books around the house, or to spend a lot of time in meetings. They told her to simply live the Christlike life at home.

One night as she was reading her Bible in the bathroom, one verse seemed to leap out at her: "You wives, be submissive to your husbands, so that some, though they do not obey the word, may be won without a word by the behavior of their wives" (1 Peter 3:1, *RSV*).

"Be submissive"! She could hardly stand to be near him, and now God said, "Be submissive"! She began praying that God would help her to love her husband again. She had a strong personality, but she quit fighting him and competing with him, and she gave up her temper tantrums.

Finally, her husband asked what had happened to her. He was amazed at the change in her attitudes. As he watched her life, he saw a real transformation. Soon he found Christ for himself. Their marriage was healed, and the drinking and drugs disappeared from their lives. Their children were also delivered from drugs, and the whole family became witnesses to Christ's saving power.

I Don't Want to Be Meek

I mentioned my friend Pilar in my book *Women of Grace* (Springfield, MO: Gospel Publishing House, 1978). She was a philosophy teacher in Argentina. It was my joy to lead her from the black pit of agnosticism to the light of Christ. She sat in my home one evening shortly before Christmas, and said, "I don't know if Walter will still love me now that I have decided to be a Christian. I will be such a different kind of person as I put Christ's principles to work in my life. I don't know if he can love the new me."

Then she laughed, "I must win him to the Lord,

but I'll have to be as clever as if I were trapping a wild animal!"

Again she laughed and said, "No, he isn't an animal, but he is so wary. I must be very wise to be able to win him without his knowing what I'm doing." She determined to win her husband by letting Christ shine through her into his darkness.

One to Another

One morning, my husband Monroe leaped out of bed when the alarm went off at 6:15. He's a fast, happy, early riser. I'm more of a night person. It seems God plans this little factor in lots of families so that both partners may learn to submit and complement each other.

Suddenly I heard a loud bang, then a groan. I called, "What happened?"

"Oh, nothing much."

I got up to see. I had just put out a big new bar of soap. It had slipped and fallen with a heavy thud right on the big vein on the top of Monroe's foot. By the time I stooped to look at it, it was swollen. Black and purple rings were spreading rapidly over the entire top of his foot. Limping around, he continued to dress. I looked at his foot again. "The better part of wisdom is for you to take some horizontal meditation today," I said.

He didn't feel all the work at the office could get done without him, but finally he gave in. I put an ice bag on his foot, and elevated it on two pillows. When I finally managed to reach a doctor, he said, "Oh yes, complete inactivity and rest for at least 24 hours." Sometimes submission is on my part. This time it was his turn to submit to my suggestion.

Second Corinthians 6:14 tells us not to be unequally yoked together with unbelievers. Christians have nothing in common with darkness. The yoke of marriage requires equality. We must be able to submit one to another, and to respect each other's judgment and ideas. God spoke to Abraham in Genesis 21:12 and told him to listen to what Sarah was saying and to obey. Yet in the New Testament it says that Sarah called Abraham "lord," which meant "master." Obviously, their relationship was a two-way street.

Reasons for Divorce

Four basic reasons are given for divorce in today's society. We will look at each of these factors in various chapters of this book:

1. Lack of communication
2. Money
3. In-laws
4. Sex

Jesus pointed out in Matthew 19:6 that marriage partners aren't two, but one. "What therefore God hath joined together, let not man put asunder." As we study further, increase our understanding, and become more aware of needs, God can help us to strengthen our good marriages, and also to heal our troubled ones.

Sharing Time

Read the entire third chapter of Colossians and Ephesians 5:19-33. With these two Scripture portions as background, explore the following questions:

1. What verbs in these Scripture passages would help us when we have disagreements?

2. If Christ dwells in our lives, what are we supposed to do about our quarrels?

3. If a couple contemplating divorce would sit down together and read these two portions, what effect could this have on them?

4. There are references to singing and songs in Colossians 3:16 and Ephesians 5:19. How can music bring healing to our hearts and help solve our problems?

5. Name some special song that has ministered healing to you.

6. Write a few words of this song in your notebook.

7. Almost all the fruit of the Spirit is found in these Scripture passages. What is the fruit of the Spirit? What difference could it make in our lives and in our attitudes toward our mates?

8. What attitude should we have toward a divorced person who comes to our church?

9. Do you know any family that hasn't been touched by divorce?

10. What modern pitfalls should we be aware of in order to help our children avoid divorce?

11. When on a trip with one acting as the navigator and the other as the pilot, aren't there times when each should submit to the other?

3

Building a Christian Home

There is a little bit of humor we share in our family. I sometimes write these words to my three children: "I'm glad you chose to come to live in our home." They often write in return: "Mommy, we made a good choice when we chose your home to live in."

Now we know it isn't possible to choose where we will be born, but we also know we have to work at establishing a home that is God-honoring. The home was the first institution. The home is the backbone of our society and our nation. Satan knows that if he can undermine the home, he has the whole nation on the skids.

Cain and Abel were products of the same home. They sat at the same table, ate the same food, and must have heard the same counsel, for they had the same parents. But Satan put jealousy and sibling rivalry into Cain's heart, and he killed his brother. That first home spawned the first murder.

Foundations

Read the Ten Commandments in Exodus 20. How many of them are a guide for the home? One person said, "The roof is the first thing needed for a home." But if we don't have a good foundation and good walls, the roof falls down. So first there has to be a foundation.

Christ must be the center and master of our home and family. This is why Ephesians 5:21-33 talks about the husband loving his wife as Jesus loved the Church and gave himself for it. So, Jesus is the head of our home. Both husband and wife are under the authority of Christ in the home, and He will reveal His will to each of them. When the children arrive and realize there is a chain of command upward toward Christ, this makes it easy to obey their parents, because the head is Christ, and they obey Him.

She Is the Crown

Proverbs 12:4 says the wife is the "crown to her husband." If she's a crown, it makes him a king! If we treat our husbands as kings, we'll find the home will be easy to shape. Proverbs 14:1 says: "Every wise woman buildeth her house: but the foolish plucketh it down with her hands." This doesn't make the husband a dictator, but rather the president, and the wife serves as vice-president. Thus, she needs to be in on the decisions and the formation of the philosophy on what kind of a home they will have. I feel that a wise woman who wants to build her home will honor her husband, respect him, and please him in every way. With a sour spirit, a nagging wife can pull her home down.

My grandmother was a wise woman. She governed her large comfortable home with a strong, firm hand. She always had some wise nuggets of counsel to give. "Never talk over problems when your man has just arrived home," she said. "Give him something good to eat first, and then when you talk, the problem can be solved. The key to a man's heart is through his stomach."

She also said, "Never meet your man at the door wearing a dirty apron. Be freshened up, showered, with neat hair and your face pretty. At least have the table set if the food isn't ready. Then he can observe that there is promise of good things to come."

Some women may work outside the home, and have different hours in relation to others in the family. But sharing time at the table is very important, so carefully organize for time together.

From the Word we see that Jesus often took time to sit down and eat with the people. The first occasion was the wedding at Cana. Some other times were at Mary and Martha's home, at Simon's home, and also at the house of Zacchaeus. After healing Peter's mother-in-law, Jesus ate as she served them. He hosted a picnic where He multiplied the loaves and fishes from the little boy's lunch. Along the seaside, He broiled fish over a fire for Peter and the disciples, and even after His resurrection He sat down and ate with two disciples at Emmaus. This intimate communion fostered bonds of family love.

What Is a Family?

Just a few years ago the accepted definition of a family was two parents living in a home together with 2.3 children. It was assumed this family lived together as a caring, sharing unit.

With the changing of our culture we are finding it more difficult to define a family. The *American*

Collegiate Dictionary defines it as "parents and their children, whether dwelling together or not." When I asked one man for a definition, he said, "A family is a fortress for the protection of love and Christian growth." Another said, "A family is a place where there is warmth and nurturing and security, with an absence of fear."

In her book *What Is a Family?* (Old Tappan, NJ: Fleming H. Revell Co., 1975), Edith Schaeffer defines a family as a "formation center for human relationships." She also speaks of a family as a center for continuity in which to create tools for starting out in life. Within the family we should help each person develop to the maximum of his/her potential—physically, mentally, spiritually, and emotionally.

Raising three children on the mission field has perhaps made me more aware of my responsibility to create a growth center where each child can realize his fullest potential. I have also realized the importance of each child having maximum freedom to become a complete, well-rounded person with dignity.

This doesn't mean we are all alike because we belong to a family, but it does mean we draw our sense of self-worth from the security of our home. In actual fact, parents soon realize that each child is very different.

Mona always said she was going to be an artist. From the age of 4, she could pick up a crayon or a pencil and a piece of paper and create a good facsimile of what she was looking at. I can't draw a good-looking stick horse, so this stretched me to be able to allow her freedom and encouragement. I remember the lessons, the paints, the rags, the artist's easel, the paint-stained shirt, and the smells of oil and turpentine emanating from her room.

Rocky was a bookworm. This was understandable, for both of his parents enjoy being students of books. Rachel enjoyed music, and that too was a part of our background so we could identify with it. Rocky always said that while his IQ was high in academic areas, Mona had a very high social IQ. Home, therefore, provided a learning experience that allowed latitude for individuality and growth, and yet all were part of one family life.

I found the following in Henry Drummond's book, *The Greatest Thing in the World* (Old Tappan, NJ: Fleming H. Revell Co., 1968):

> The people who influence you are people who believe in you. In an atmosphere of suspicion men shrivel up; but in that atmosphere (of belief and love) they expand, and find encouragement and educative fellowship.

I think a family is a setting in which we can be ourselves to *say, do, become,* and *reach our goals,* and still be *loved.*

The Breakdown

There are many factors prevalent in today's society which are undermining the family and causing its breakdown. In the book *Personal Marriage Contract* (Dallas, TX: OK Street Inc., 1976), John Whitaker, M.D., actually proposes a contract for 2 to 5 years, stating that the declaration of commitment in marriage would be only for that period of time. He calls many of the cherished Christian mores "myths." He says there are no absolute guarantees; *now* is the only real forever.

This underscores the fact that some teachers in our secular schools are presenting marriage as an option one may choose if he wishes. They are taking the sacred part out of marriage by saying it is only human. This doesn't create a warm family unit where a child can learn to love as he grows.

The End of Marriage

If we are aware of what is going on around us, we will hear alarming statements from the various media. In lectures, newspapers, and magazines, and on secular college campuses, an end to marriage is often proposed. According to one public statement: "The end of marriage is a necessary condition for the liberation of women; therefore, we must encourage women to leave their husbands and not live individually with men." If you listen to these propagators of insidious philosophies, you will hear them insisting that the best thing for children is to take them away from their families. Couples are told that those who wish to live in equal partnership should abolish the institution of legal marriage.

Along with this teaching is a return to female religions and an upsurge of witchcraft. There is now freedom to practice witchcraft openly, and there are even schools for witches. This is a satanic attack on today's families, and we need to be *aware* of it so we won't be deceived by the smooth talk of equality and rights.

Kinds of Families

There are many kinds of families today. The conjugal family unit living together is called by some the *nuclear* family.

27

Sociologists talk about the *extended* family, which includes grandparents, uncles, aunts, and others in the wider family circle. The extended family was important in Biblical times, and right here is where we find our children hurting so much today. Often they are moved around so frequently that they don't know the other members of their extended family.

The *fractured* family is the one wounded by divorce or by the inattentiveness or absence of one parent. This wounds the family members—both the children and the parents.

The *blended* family is one in which two parents bring children from a former marriage, and blend them into a situation where they become "yours," "mine," and "ours."

The *free-form* family is one where the children can choose to go with either parent after the divorce, moving back and forth at will. No one has definite custody. Part of the time they can all live together and share responsibilities, although not officially joined in marriage.

The *single-parent family* is a growing segment of our society. A high percentage of children are now being raised in single-parent homes. This may be caused by the death of a partner, divorce, the imprisonment of a mate, a business that calls for the extended absence of one parent over long periods of time, or a parent who opts to retain a child born out of wedlock. Whatever the cause, the church must be understanding toward these familes who need acceptance and help.

The *mended* family is one where parents work out their problems with the Word of God. It takes humility to be willing to look for help.

If we are aware of the problems, we can keep our family from getting sick. We can become a *welded* family in which the glue of love, compassion, and loyalty holds members together through all crises. We can have faith to be kept. "Thou shalt be saved, *and thy house*" (Acts 16:31) is God's promise to His people.

Our children have helped to weld our family together with the cards they have given us through the years. Their cards contain words of sharing, joy, hope, understanding, happy times, listening, and caring. I have saved many of these cards, and while looking through them I found one titled "A Happy Family Is an Earlier Heaven." It expresses such a lovely sentiment that I'd like to share it with you.

A Happy Family Is an Earlier Heaven

What a precious gift
To be a part of a warm loving family,
To be supported, comforted in time of trouble,
To share the little triumphs and great joys.

The children have often mentioned that memories of our times of sharing together kept them during the years we were apart. Being accepted, loved, and respected as a person is the greatest treasure anyone could receive.

I've always said my father left us no great inheritance of wealth, but the inheritance he left us was something no one could buy. It was sharing, understanding, and listening. He knew how to listen, and we passed this on to our children.

Family is a beautiful word. A family is a God-inspired concept, and a reservoir of strength.

Play Together

When remembering their childhood, I have heard some people say, "Yes, we took time to work together and pray together, but I have no memories of ever playing together."

Our family kept Friday nights open to play together. We made popcorn, played games, went caroling, sang, and showed family slides. We learned to be good "sports" because we played together.

Family for the Solitary

"God setteth the solitary in families" (Psalm 68:6). The family unit brings healing.

"Blessed be the Lord, who daily loadeth us with benefits" (Psalm 68:19). One benefit is our family.

Jesus came "to heal the brokenhearted, to preach deliverance to the captives, and recovering of sight to the blind, to set at liberty them that are bruised" (Luke 4:18).

The Choice

In Deuteronomy 30:15,16 Moses reminds the people of the important commands to love the Lord, walk in His ways, and keep His commandments. Accordingly, the people are promised that they will live, multiply, and be blessed if they are obedient. Obedience to God is also the best way to strengthen our families.

In Joshua 24:14,15 Joshua challenges the people in a farewell speech by saying: "Fear the Lord, and serve him in sincerity and in truth; . . . choose you this day whom ye will serve; . . . as for me and my house, we will serve the Lord." We need to make this choice for our family today. Serve God, read the

Word, pray, meet with God's people in worship and service, and live right!

... And Thy House

We know the story from Acts 16:25-31 about Paul and Silas singing in prison. The prisoners heard them, and God sent an earthquake to deliver them. Paul called out to the jailer not to commit suicide because all the prisoners were there. The jailer was so astonished that he said, "Sirs, what must I do to be saved?" Paul answered, "Believe on the Lord Jesus Christ, and thou shalt be saved, *and thy house.*"

Verses 31-34 indicate that the jailer was the authority in his home. Because he took the first step, his whole family accepted the Lord.

In different countries where I have spoken, women have come to me after the meetings and asked, "May I touch you? Since your three children are all serving God, can God save my husband? Can He save my children? What must I do for my family? How do I start? Where does the healing come from? Help me pray!"

God gives us His promise: "*. . . and thy house.*"

Foundation Stones for a Good Home

1. Sincere love—1 Corinthians 13
2. Virtue—2 Peter 1:5-8
3. Commitment—Proverbs 31:11 (Trust is a two-way street)
4. Loyalty—Colossians 3:18-23
5. Mutual respect—1 Peter 3:7
6. Sincerity—Titus 2
7. Cooperation—Ephesians 5:21-23

Sharing Time

1. Ask your children what they would like to change about their home. It might give you some good guidelines. Can we be transparent?

2. Plan to compliment every family member. Write down some of the compliments you are going to use, so you won't forget.

3. Find some time to play a game together.

4. Read Psalm 121 together.

5. Memorize Ephesians 4:32. Try doing what it says.

6. Plan a special meal. Light some candles; use your good china; arrange some flowers. See what kind of reactions you get.

4

Keeping Communications Open

Communications is considered such an art that college degrees are offered in the subject. Yet some of us assume that because we speak the same language we are sure to be able to communicate.

A recently married couple called home long-distance after the honeymoon. I asked them, "Have you had your first argument?"

"How could you know?" they asked in surprise.

"Well," I said, "there are bound to be some differences when two individuals start learning to be one."

Can you imagine what the argument was about? It was over how many towels to use! One wanted a clean towel after every shower. The other said, "No, that's too much washing; too much soap; too much water; that's not necessary."

They pouted about it for a while, then decided they would have clean towels twice a week.

Another young couple was in the process of arranging their wedding gifts around the house. They organized the kitchen, and then decided to hang the lovely paintings they had received. Most of the day was spent disagreeing over whether the paintings should be up near the molding or down at eye level. Have you noticed where some people hang their mirrors? I'm short, so very often I can't see myself in them. But then others have to stoop to see into mine!

The Little Foxes

Solomon learned much from experience. He knew it was the little foxes that spoiled the vines. And it's often the little disagreements that start the root of bitterness growing. You will remember that the list of basic reasons for divorce includes lack of communication, money, in-laws, and sexual problems. In this chapter we'll talk about making a conscious effort at successful communication.

We marry for a lot of reasons. We see others doing it; we're afraid to live alone; we don't want to be single; or we meet someone who makes the butterflies flutter in our hearts. But often we don't take the time to talk, to ask important questions, and to really understand each other. Before marrying someone, we should consider questions such as: What are our goals? What is our family background? What is the spiritual commitment of our potential partner?

If we are Christians we may say, "We're praying about it." But this is not enough. We need to talk, to communicate, and to share.

Be of One Accord

In Amos 3:3 we read, "Can two walk together, except they be agreed?" We need to speak the same language, share the same faith, and have similar goals. To understand each other takes time. Communication is a two-way street.

A man in his seventies went to the doctor for a

physical examination and was told he was in excellent condition.

He was asked, "What is your secret?"

He replied, "When my wife and I were married 50 years ago we agreed that when she saw a fault in me she would be quiet, and when I lost my temper because of a fault in her I would take a walk. Perhaps my good health is due to the fact that all these years I've lived mainly an outdoor life."

Sounds crazy, doesn't it? Marriage is the only war where the enemies sleep in the same bed. When we were married my husband and I made a decision never to say, "It's your fault," when things went wrong. Rather, we would share decisions and their consequences as "ours." The commitment to share consequences calls for open communication in decisionmaking.

"Be ye angry, and sin not: let not the sun go down upon your wrath" (Ephesians 4:26). This means that if there have been any differences or harsh words in your communications during the day, it is good to make up with each other and reach a time of peaceful forgiveness before going to sleep.

When Joe and Mary play a piano duet, the harmony doesn't come without effort. The duet of a perfect marriage also requires practice in tempo, rhythm, touch, and expression—whether it is to be soft, loud, slow, or fast. Neither one possesses all qualities within himself, but together we complement each other. This produces harmony.

Nonverbal Communication

Egocentricity can bring about incompatibility. We are headed for trouble when we are only concerned about our own ways and our own wants—when we take the "I've got to be me" attitude.

Someone remarked facetiously concerning a couple, "They separated because of incompatibility. He lost his income, and she lost her 'patability.'"

I have a warm memory of Daddy hugging Mother and giving her a little pat. This is the kind of two-way communication in a home that is healthy for children to see. It is nonverbal communication that says the home is alive and the marriage is secure. Children understand and benefit from this kind of communication.

Reassure Each Other

If a woman asks a man if he loves her, the reply will often be, "You know I do. Don't I bring my paycheck home? Don't I pay the rent?" Sure he does, but a woman needs to be told and to be reassured. She needs verbal as well as nonverbal communication.

At the door of the church I overheard a woman say, "Tomorrow my husband leaves, then everything will get back to normal." I wondered, *How can that be?* I have to be alone quite frequently while my husband travels to teaching seminars, so I couldn't imagine a woman *wanting* to be alone.

The woman continued, "Yes, for 20 years he's been a traveling salesman. But not long ago, he broke an ankle, and he's been home for several weeks recuperating. Now, everything I do is wrong. He doesn't like the way I raise the children. He doesn't like the way I've painted the house. Of course, he wasn't here to help me, but now he's finding fault. When he's working again we'll be able to stand having him home for the weekends."

Wow! I thought. *Now there's a real lack of communication.*

This week a woman told me, "I'm retiring from my job. My colleagues held a neat party for me. But I've been home 1 week now, and that's enough. I've got to find something to do to get out of the house and away from him." She can't stand that daily proximity. Maybe it would be good just to sit down and relax together, to take a walk or be quiet together, and to let the "radar" start again.

One young friend of mine observed this about his parents, who also happen to be close friends of ours, "Now that we children have grown up and married, my parents act like honeymooners." This is a great compliment.

There is an old saying, "Man must work from sun to sun, but woman's work is never done." It's true, a woman can always find something more to do. But sometimes this is a pretext for not spending time together. Perhaps she keeps wiping up spots in the kitchen, rewaxes the floor, or stays in the shower until he goes to sleep. Then there is no communication, and no time for physical intimacy.

Coals of Fire

One woman told her minister about her unsaved husband and asked for counsel on how to have a Christian home. The preacher said, "In the Bible it says to heap coals of fire on his head. Have you tried that?"

She replied, "Oh no, sir. But I tried hitting him over the head with a skillet and that hasn't worked." We laugh, but to build our house well we must be wise.

Don't attack the character of your mate. Don't say, "You *never* listen." "You *always* do this." "You are mean." "You are stingy." "You don't understand me." These are judgmental statements. Be careful of the words *never* and *always*. They are words that bruise.

My daddy came from a broken home. He told us how his mother would clam up and sulk in an effort to get grandfather to feel sorry for her. My grandparents wouldn't speak to each other for weeks, although they shared the same table and bed. Grandfather finally left her, and Daddy became the man of the house in a single-parent family when he was only in the sixth grade.

Keep Growing

I read a book about a couple who had problems. I'll always remember what the husband said: "We grew apart—you stood still." It is so important to keep growing, to keep reading, to keep sharing ideas, and not to communicate only with mere clichés. Pray together that you will always feel free to be open and communicate. Don't take each other for granted.

Frequently, I hear women say, "Now that the children are gone, we are strangers. We don't have anything in common." This shows the need for growth. Take some courses. Read books. Maybe you should go back to school to keep your mind alive. Try sharing some television programs and then talk them over. Does he enjoy baseball? Learn to understand and enjoy something *he* likes. Share music together. Go for a walk. Go to an art exhibition. You can even share some of the courses he's taking or some of the books he's exploring. Grow together, not apart. We have to make a conscious effort to grow.

Seek counseling help before you let your marriage die. There are many marriage enrichment seminars available to those who will make the effort. Sometimes men feel threatened with the idea of such a course of action, and it is not always easy to involve them in a situation they might see as making themselves vulnerable.

A woman needs to talk and to chat. Sometimes a woman who is feeling lonely will say, "I can't get his wall down. He won't listen; he just puts the newspaper in front of him. He clams up or goes off to play golf. He just doesn't want to talk." Maybe it's the constant whining, complaining, or empty chitchat that drives him out the door. What is the level of your speech in relation to his? Perhaps that's why it's so often a monologue.

Occasionally it's good for a woman to have a woman friend with whom to share her own feelings about various problems. This can be a source of relief for frustrating situations. Then, in her communication time with her husband, she may try some new ideas, share her thoughts about a book, or discuss something fresh from the Bible. But she must be careful not to hit him over the head with it.

There are many good books written to help keep communication open. Among other things, they suggest a woman should ask about her husband's day, and about his feelings. Then she should *listen* to him. Maybe he's trying to communicate something more than his words convey.

God had a great idea in marriage. The woman was to be a helper, and to be able to understand her man. I can imagine Adam's reaction when he woke up from his surgery. "What is this? Am I dreaming? This is someone new!" Then they began to communicate and to learn about each other. That term *knew*, in Genesis 4:1, implies many facets—the physical sex act, and also the feelings, goals, wishes, and desires in the heart of each other.

We need to keep both eyes open before marriage and one eye closed afterwards—closed to faults and weaknesses we may have seen before but accepted with both eyes open.

My husband and I often say to each other, "I like you. I like being with you. I like the way you do things. I like the thoughts you think. I like the atmosphere you bring into our home."

If we would accept the positive things about each other and minimize the negative, we'd find it easier to communicate. Too many people build walls instead of bridges. I like the sentiments expressed by a popular song which speaks of getting to know one another, all about one another, and liking one another, until you become each other's "cup of tea."

Once when we were staying with friends, the husband told us, "We've watched how you communicate. When one of you is speaking and the other wishes to interrupt, since you are holding hands, you simply tap gently with one finger on the other's wrist. There's no need for breaking in; the other one knows."

We hadn't even realized it ourselves; it was something we had learned by working at communication and courtesy with each other.

40

Keeping Communications Open

Here are some references from God's Word for you to consider as you work toward improving communication.

1. Communion—in prayer (James 5:16)
2. Communication (Ephesians 4:29-32)
3. Conversation—a two-way street (Deuteronomy 6:5-9)
4. Contentment—great gain (Philippians 4:11)
5. Confidence—mutual trust (Proverbs 31:11)
6. Courage (Psalm 91:4-6)
7. Consideration—hospitality (Romans 12:13)
8. Companionship—togetherness (Philippians 2:25)
9. Comprehension—of one accord (Amos 3:3)
10. Commitment (Colossians 3:17-24)
11. Crown of the home—her husband isn't ashamed of her (Proverbs 12:4)

Communication Is a Process

1. It must flow both ways.
2. Listening is of vital importance in communicating.
3. We communicate with the spirit, a squeeze of the hand, a look of the eye, a quirk of the mouth, or a tone of voice.
4. Verbal and nonverbal communication must agree to be understood. Do your lips smile while your eyes "send daggers"?
5. Realize that hostile silence can be dangerous.
    a. Bitterness can grow out of sulkiness (Hebrews 12:15).
    b. Bottled up resentment is a dangerous explosive.

41

c. Psychological barbed wire fences promote withdrawal.

6. Wise silence is golden; don't suffocate your mate with constant chatter.

7. Be open; take your defenses down; submit.

8. Keep dialogue open, and don't be guilty of holding a monologue.

> Ephesians 4:26—let not the sun go down upon your wrath.
>
> Proverbs 15:1—a soft answer turns away wrath.
>
> Proverbs 16:32—be slow to anger.
>
> Proverbs 18:4—words are as deep waters.

9. Be sensitive to feedback from the other person.

10. Use empathy—walk in his shoes, and feel with him. If you're not going to be home as planned, use the telephone. Don't keep your mate waiting and wondering if you're hurt or with someone else.

11. Show appreciation. Before marriage there were flowers, cards, and evenings out for dinner. How about a "thank you" for his thoughtfulness now, rather than taking it for granted?

12. Make eye contact; give your mate your attention.

13. Encourage communication. Cut out articles from magazines and newspapers which you know your partner won't have time to read. Your spouse may share something from a book. Keep tuned in to each other.

14. Write to each other. A nice card or a note is always appreciated. I find a note under my pillow each time Monroe travels.

Sharing Time

To show some of the pitfalls of communication,

try this exercise. Stand back to back with another person. Take a large piece of paper and a pencil. Let the other person look at a graph or illustration and give you instructions on how to draw it. "Put a line; draw a circle. Now make a square—a cloud." After you finish, look at the original picture and compare it to the one you've drawn. How did you do? Are they similar?

Life is like that. We think we're communicating, but maybe we're just talking without being understood. Maybe no one's listening.

Talk this over. What could have made your communication clearer? This can be discussed in your class or group. Then try this exercise at home with your mate.

1. Choose an article or Scripture passage and talk about it together. Then read it together. Does it really say what you thought it did when you first discussed it?

2. Offer to read to your mate while you travel, or in another situation. This can stimulate discussion.

3. We communicate on different levels. Look at the communication examples below. Make some of your own for discussion purposes. On what level are you sharing?

Level 5—Clichés*
"How are you?"   "Fine."

Level 4—Report Facts
"How are the kids?"   "Out of school."

---

*Adapted from H. Norman Wright, *Communication: Key to Your Marriage*, p. 69. Copyright 1974 by Regal Books Division, G/L Publications.

43

Level 3—Ideas and Judgments

"It's too cold to go to the picnic."

"But I've already fixed the food!"

Level 2—Feelings and Emotions

"I can't stand all those kids screaming in the car. We'll stay home!"

"They'll be disappointed."

Level 1—Open, Truthful Communication

"I'd rather work on my hobby. I need time to be alone."

"Maybe just taking time to be together will be the best holiday."

How did your dialogue turn out? Were you just saying clichés or were you communicating?

5

Teaching the Young Women

My husband and I went to the home of a young Latin American pastor and his new bride.

"Come in. Welcome to our home," the bride said. And together they lifted the door on its sagging hinges, and then lifted it again to close it behind us. She was radiant.

"This is our first home. We were fortunate to find a place to rent."

My eyes adjusted to the semidarkness, and I looked around while smiling and chatting.

The table was set and ready. We sat on some rickety wicker chairs, and I couldn't help noticing the cracks between the floor boards. A cat wandered in and brushed against a basket, knocking it over. Whoops! Underneath was a hole big enough for a rat to crawl through. The walls were freshly covered with old newspapers, but they were clean. The smell of stale cigar smoke came right through the cardboard walls from the neighbor's. It was very cold, so I was glad for my woolen Bolivian poncho and my leather boots.

As she poured the hot tea, the wife said, "I didn't know how to do anything but work in an office, so my husband is teaching me how to cook. This is my first jam."

It was made from bitter oranges and tasted tart and good, and we spread it on crackers. Their eyes were shining with joy and contentment, and the afternoon passed quickly as we shared their vision of the ministry God would give them together. Their attitude was, "Together we are invincible."

"To Be Content"

I was reminded that Paul said it right when he said, "I have learned . . . to be content" (see Philippians 4:11-13). No one is born content. We are all born grasping. But we must learn to be content with a little or a lot. Contentment is the most basic grace for building a Christian home. It's not the color of the walls, nor the size of the rooms; it's the outliving of contentment. Victor Hugo said: "A house built of logs, stones, beams, and piers can last but a short time, but a home built of loving deeds and words stands a thousand years."

Many have asked me how I can stand to live in Miami after living overseas for 25 years. My answer is: "I have a basic philosophy of life: to be content wherever I am." Whether it's an Indian village, a Bible school dorm, or a house in Miami, it is contentment that makes a house a home.

The Bible says a lot about contentment (Philippians 4:11). Here are a few passages for you to study: "Godliness with contentment is great gain" (1 Timothy 6:6). "Be content with such things as ye have" (Hebrews 13:5). "Be content with your wages" (Luke 3:14). Titus 2 tells us how to make a home. Read this chapter in Titus and see how many things older women are instructed to teach the younger women! One of the problems causing the disintegration of homes today is that we haven't taken time to obey this Scripture passage; to teach.

Teach the young women to be wise. A wise woman builds her home and rests in the knowledge that her husband is the head of the home. She relaxes in allowing him to be the head. They are supportive of each other. He doesn't feel threatened because she reinforces his headship, and he is also supportive of his wife.

I like it when my husband says, "I treat my wife as a person."

"To Love Their Husbands"

Is it possible girls don't know how to love their husbands? Yes. I heard a girl say recently: "I grew up in a family of boys. We had lots of competition and wrangling. I hadn't been married long before I realized I was wrecking my marriage by nagging my husband about everything he did. After reading the book *Women of Grace,* I realized I wasn't growing in God. We started praying together, and it's working wonders in helping me to love my husband."

A wise woman lets her husband know she loves him. My mother liked green beans fixed with bacon. Daddy liked yellow wax beans with cream sauce. So we could tell which one Mother was favoring by the way the beans were fixed!

Wash-and-wear shirts help give us more hours in the day for other things, but occasionally, ironing the shirts he likes best will produce a special twinkle of joy in his eyes.

"To Love Their Children"

Is it hard to love children? Why is there so much

47

child abuse today? When I looked down into the face of my granddaughter Larisa Michelle, and saw those bright eyes and beautiful round head, it was so easy to love her. Then when she cried and screamed all night with a tummy ache, I realized we have to *learn* love. Some young mothers can't be patient with 6 weeks of colic. They are practicing being mothers and have so much to learn!

God always sends the new baby to the inexperienced parent! We must learn to love and not to react without thinking. An integral part of loving our children is correcting them. If a child does wrong, tell him, "I love you, but I don't like what you did." Reason with him.

When I was finally able to visit in my daughter's home and get acquainted with my beautiful granddaughter Kristi, she was 14 months old. She had never seen me before, so we were getting to know each other. It was -20°, and since she had a cold, I stayed home from church with her. We rocked and sang, and then she wanted to get down and walk around. She decided to touch the ceramic donkey and crystal on the coffee table.

"Kristi, your mommy has said that's a no-no!"

She looked at me with her big brown eyes, and held my gaze as she again extended her hand to touch. "No, Kristi," I said.

Then she slapped at me. I finally held her hands and we walked to find a cookie to divert her thoughts. But the incident showed me how clever and how naughty a child of my own blood can be. I could have simply laughed it off, but I know that to love we must also correct.

Some say of their child, "He screams at me! He hits me! I'm devastated!" Often at home, on the school grounds, or at other times we may excuse their temper tantrum with, "Well, he's just like Uncle Dudley. He used to scream like that." But to love we must also correct.

"To Be Discreet, Chaste"

We are to be self-controlled and pure. We are to dress without being ostentatious and without drawing unnecessary attention to ourselves. I have seen girls hitchhiking at night wearing tight shorts. They are advertising an impression about themselves by the clothes they wear. They are asking for trouble.

We can be chaste in the way we walk by not swinging our hips and giving the "come-on" with our eyes. "The heart of her husband doth safely trust in her" (Proverbs 31:11). My husband travels internationally in his teaching ministry. Some years he's away from home as much as 200 days. The trust between us is a two-way street. He trusts me and I trust him. I know he is discreet, careful, and upright.

To Be "Keepers at Home"

Homemaking is an art. Chapter 11 is full of homemaking hints, but let me give an illustration here.

We were enjoying a short furlough one time when Rocky said, "Now that Mommy is here, we'll have bread-and-butter pickles." It did not occur to him that we would be too busy or too transient to take time out to make pickles. Making pickles was part of "home" for him.

So, we made bread-and-butter pickles together. It was a happy time. The girls sliced cucumbers and helped wash the jars. There's something wonderful about the aroma of fresh pickle vinegar. It wafted over the wall to the neighbors and they wanted to know how to make them. Bread-and-butter pickles are a favorite choice for Thanksgiving and Christmas, and a pint jar of them decorated with a ribbon even makes a welcome Christmas gift.

Let me share my recipe with you:

Jane's Bread-and-Butter Pickles

Thinly slice 1 gallon of cucumbers. Add 6 tablespoons salt. Cover with water. Let stand overnight, and rinse in the morning.

12 sliced onions	
1 red pepper	Bring to a boil.
3 pints vinegar	Lay the sliced
4 cups sugar	"cukes" in the
1 tablespoon celery seed	hot vinegar solution. (Do not boil.)
2 tablespoons mustard seed	
2 teaspoons turmeric	Seal in sterilized jars.

To Be "Good"

This means we should be a model to others by our manner of living. There is always a real opportunity in the home to demonstrate being patient, kind, and forgiving, and not to become cross or retaliatory.

After her women's group had studied the fruit of patience, my sister went home to make fresh rhubarb sauce. The phone rang, and she quickly put the bowl on top of the refrigerator. When she opened the refrigerator later, the bowl fell off. Rhubarb sauce splattered all over the refrigerator, on our father, and on the floor! She was able to put her lesson in patience into practice!

Our daughter Sherry wrote from Argentina about an opportunity she had to practice patience. Just before leaving the house to teach a class, she picked up a 2-quart bottle of cooking oil. It slipped out of her hands, broke into a thousand pieces on the marble floor, and spread a lake of oil all over her kitchen. Can we be calm under such circumstances? Or do we lash out at our family? "It's your fault! You tripped me!" Shh . . . shh. . . .

We should also be aware of the dangers inherent in such things as horoscopes and the occult. We should concentrate on reading good books and magazines. We should think good thoughts (Philippians 4:8). We should turn off filthy television programs and prevent their evil influences from pervading our homes.

To Be "Obedient to Their Own Husbands"

We teach this by our example. Thus, we can "adorn the doctrine of God" (Titus 2:10). A woman can pray for her husband to be a good, wise head of the household, and then relax in dependence on God to direct him. First Corinthians 11:11 says: "In the Lord, however, woman is not independent of man, nor is man independent of woman" (*New International Version*). It's a two-way street. The man is to love his wife as his own body, and to pray for her. The wife is to be obedient. Together they fashion their home according to God's design.

Titus 2:3-5 shows us the need to reinforce each member of our family with these truths. We must be

51

supportive, and help them by demonstrating a pattern of good works in our own manner of speaking and "being." What we are, and what we do, influences our families far beyond what we say.

Don't degrade the character of your family members with accusations in front of others. Living by the rule of Ephesians 4:32 will help you to make your home a happy haven for your family: "Be ye kind one to another, tender-hearted, forgiving one another, even as God for Christ's sake hath forgiven you."

Sharing Time

1. According to Titus 2:3-12, what values should Christian women develop?

2. How can we be discreet and chaste examples at home?

3. Titus 2:9 says we shouldn't "answer again." Do you know someone who has a problem in this area? How could it wreck a marriage?

4. Make a list of the ways you can adorn the doctrine of God (v. 10).

5. Verse 12 says we should live godly, sober lives today. How is this possible?

6. Are there any factors in our lives that need changing before we can be obedient to verse 12?

7. What effect does careful conversation have on the atmosphere of our home?

Sing together the beautiful prayer song by Bill and Gloria Gaither, "Come, Holy Spirit." You will be blessed by the beautiful words.

6

Showing the Way

Our daughter Rachel wrote home from college and said, "I'm taking this course in 'Family and the Home,' and it's uncanny. The book was just published, but you've done everything right! How could you have known these things when this is a new course in colleges?"

"Well," we chuckled, "we knew those things because our textbook has always been the *Book* of books."

This chapter could be expanded to a full college course, because it covers a lifetime of living. But we'll only point to some of the secrets we have discovered in the areas of teaching, training, and trusting.

When I had a decision to make my father used to say, "We have trained you, and now we trust you with the choice. The decision is yours." This was long before all the wonderful books on raising children were available. It was before the days of democratic homes (the father was still the autocratic figure). But it was a practical way to train me. I responded to his gentleness, and I wouldn't have offended my daddy for anything. I didn't want to hurt him. It has helped to keep me strong in the face of temptations and decisions throughout my life.

A mouse may live in a cookie jar, but that doesn't make him a cookie. And just because a child is born to Christian parents, it doesn't automatically mean that his soul is saved. It takes teaching, training, instructing, talking, setting an example, loving, and also disciplining.

Let's see what Scripture says. Read Deuteronomy 6:5-9, and note the beautiful progression of instructions.

Teach the Word

1. "When thou sittest in thine house." We must take the opportunity to make comparisons, instill values, and guide the thinking in the home.

2. "When thou walkest by the way." We must teach the Word while traveling, while at a picnic, while riding a bicycle or a bus, and while driving the car. Instead of sitting at the stoplight, and growling, "That idiot! Why did he make a left turn?" we are to be patient and to pray for him. Maybe he's had a bad day. We must remember that we are teaching attitudes; even at stoplights.

3. "When thou liest down." Nighttime is a good opportunity to teach the Word. As you tuck the children in, and as you go to your own room, you can commit your family to the Lord. Psalm 4:8 says: "I will both lay me down in peace, and sleep: for thou, Lord, only makest me dwell in safety." Rest in the Lord.

4. "When thou risest up." The mercies of the Lord are new and fresh every morning (Lamentations 3:22,23). Psalm 118:24 says: "This is the day which the Lord hath made; we will rejoice and be glad in it." Memorize this Scripture verse with your

family; say it every day. I heard one woman say she didn't want a dishwasher. Doing the dishes after a meal was "togetherness time" with her children—a time to talk to them, train them, and *listen* to them.

Deuteronomy 6:5,6 says: "And thou shalt love the Lord thy God with all thine heart, and with all thy soul, and with all thy might. And these words, which I command thee this day, shall be in thine heart."

I'm convinced that if we really do love the Lord with our emotions, our understanding, our willpower, and our strength, our children are going to know it, and it will be easier for them to love God. We are transparent at home.

It's "Caught," Not "Taught"

Our daughter Mona taught at a Bible school in Panama shortly after she graduated from college. She was living by faith "on a shoestring," and wrote that she didn't have enough money to buy stamps for her letters. I replied in a letter that I was sure God didn't want her to be in need, and that someone could help her—she didn't have to live wholly by faith. She wrote back to remind me that it was in our own home that she had learned to live by faith. Faith is "caught," not "taught."

In verses 8 and 9 we are told to bind the Word of God on our arm and between our eyes, and to write it on the doorposts of our homes. The Jewish people wrote out verses of Scripture and put them into little leather boxes which they tied on their foreheads and arms. In that way, they carried the Word around with them. But God wants us to write the Scriptures in our hearts through reading, memorizing, and meditating upon them. Then they will influence our attitudes and our entire way of life.

Do your neighbors know you are a Christian? We don't have to paint a sign advertising this fact on our fences, but our neighbors should be able to tell by our home, our conversation, our friendliness, our helpfulness, and our children. We don't need to advertise it with a bumper sticker, but they should be able to see Christ in us by the way we drive.

No Pecking

The mother duck held her head high as she moved across the road. A young "teenaged" duckling moved in front of her. I stopped my car and waited for them to finish crossing the road. The duckling was nearly as tall as his mother. He presented a slender and dignified appearance with his head high, turning neither to the right nor to the left. The mother duck didn't go ahead of him or prod him, but she kept moving close behind him. She sheltered him so he would not dash backwards, but move safely on to the other side.

Watching them, I thought, *This is really what training means.* Early in your child's experience you begin to talk to him, to show him, and to teach him. For a while you walk ahead of your child, just like the mother duck does at first with her soft, fuzzy ducklings. Then the time comes for the young ones to walk on their own, but you still walk near enough for them to feel the warmth of your shelter, your encouragement, and your care for them. No pecking now! They know what you expect of them, and they walk a straight line, but they like to feel that you are there. It costs time to be near, but this is a delicate stage in the training cycle.

I heard John and Tib Sherrill say that although they are busy writers and editors, they always tried to see to it that at least one of them was home when their children returned from school. This policy has paid off for them and the well-being of their home.

Possibly you work outside the home and it's difficult to be there when your children come home from school. But be sure you know where your children are, and that they know exactly how they can reach you by telephone.

My friend Elva Hoover told me that when she married into a ready-made family she quit her job in order to stay home for 5 full years until the youngest child was in junior high. She cherishes the memory of one of the boy's remarks, "It's so nice to come home (in winter) and not find the house dark."

I knew where I would find my mother each afternoon when I walked home from school. She would be downstairs in a warm little room on her knees. This proximity is important as we teach and train our children.

Proximity

At the Miami Seaquarium I watched a mother dolphin as she taught her baby how to perform. She showed him how to jump, glide, and walk on his tail. The mother performed all the steps, with the baby following along very closely. At times, the mother would turn and give the baby a whack with her tail if he didn't stay close enough. I talked with the trainer. She said the mother actually teaches the baby dolphin most of the performance before the trainer takes over. The mother dolphin teaches, trains, and demonstrates.

Our children need closeness with their parents. They need to know that they are doing the right thing and that they are accepted. They need to be reinforced with praise, and lovingly disciplined when necessary.

I remember the years when my three children sat on the front bench in church while I played the piano. I trained them by hand signals or a nod of my head. As they grew up and sat in the congregation with their friends, I always knew where they were and what they were doing.

One time our son Rocky said, "I don't think I'll ever be able to raise a child."

"Why is that?" I asked.

"Well, I can't snap my fingers."

I laughed, remembering that the children always said I had eyes in the back of my head. This proximity and the constant awareness of my children and their needs, was my responsibility during those teaching and training years.

Each child must come to realize his own worth and dignity as a complete person. As we open the Bible to read and pray together, we form a memory that will never be erased from the hearts and minds of our children. At the end of chapter 10 is a list of helps for the family altar.

Part of training children is allowing them to actually do the things we have been teaching them about. Some mothers say, "Oh, they make such a mess in my kitchen. I'd rather wash my own dishes than to have to mop up all that water." But when we discourage the child who wants to help, we are teaching him that he isn't worth anything, and that he has nothing to contribute. Incidental teaching of this type will also create a memory a child will never forget. When you cut a fresh rosebud, it withers before it has time to open into a lovely flower. Time must be taken to instruct and train. Yes, and they can mop up the water they spill.

We had times of cookie baking at Christmas. Each child chose his favorite cookie batter. We worked together. What a mess that kitchen was—flour on the floor; nutshells scattered; bits of raw dough lying around! But we didn't finish until the crisp brown cookies were carried on a plate to Daddy for him to taste. Then we cleaned up the kitchen together. Togetherness is important.

Vacation Time

Vacation should be a time of special anticipation, but many parents dread these days. This is especially true if the parents are "screamers"—both the children and the parents will be worn out. These extra hours together should be used to develop a closer relationship.

Vacation is an unregimented period of time that is exclusively yours to train and teach your children. It is a time to have picnics and to go swimming, fishing, or biking. Even if you can't take a trip, take time—time to teach them how to plant a garden and watch the miracle of life and growth. Take time for sewing or handcrafts. Take time to read together, to share, to play, and to soak up life. Life with the children is so short, and very soon they're gone.

We have to be willing to work at ideas for vacation time. We can plan scavenger hunts, model with clay, play music, and enjoy special games or sports. Look for things you can do together. Too often I've seen parents grow tired of screaming, plop their child down in front of the television with a plate of hot dogs, chips, and junk food, and say, "It's going to be a *long* summer!"

When the days get hot, we must discipline ourselves to control our voice and temper. Don't scream, "You *never* make your bed!" "You *never* pick up your socks!" "You never. . ." is often a self-fulfilling prophecy. Avoid it. Show them how to make their beds. Occasionally help them pick things up. This togetherness will help them respect you, and it's not nearly as debilitating as screaming.

Trusting

What can we do when we see problems in the lives of our children's friends that could be a bad influence on our own children? We cannot always withdraw ourselves or our children from contact with these friends; rather, we must train our children, and then trust them to choose right.

I remember how I sheltered our children with my presence, and how I prayed behind them at the altar as they sought the Lord. But the time comes when we must trust them to choose right. We shouldn't cut down their friends. We shouldn't open their mail. We shouldn't show shock if they do share secrets with us. If we lack wisdom, let us ask God for it. He will help us (James 1:5).

A woman admits, "I didn't really want my children." Then she wonders why they are in trouble, on drugs, rebellious, and not serving the Lord. She has created their insecurity by her own testimony before them.

An experiment was conducted in 400 homes to measure the time fathers spent with their small children. It averaged out to 37 seconds a day! But those same children may watch as much as 54 hours of television a week. So who is giving them their models of morality? Who is forming their values and ideals? If we really care about what our children watch on TV and what is influencing them, let us give them more time and training during their formative years. The television has an "off" button, too.

Time together with your children must be *quality* time. When our children were small, my husband was away for many months in missions ministry. But we always included Daddy in our thinking, conversation, and activities. Our three children never really felt that he was away. This takes special effort on the part of the wife and mother. She can't give in to self-pity and say, "Poor me, I'm always alone. Poor children with no father; he's off doing God's business." We need to be very careful of this "feeling-sorry-for-yourself" syndrome. After all, there are other Christian families who are also busy working for the Kingdom.

Rocky wrote from Argentina that he remembers how we provided *quality* time for the family. We played games, made popcorn, and talked over ideas and books. He included a list of his memories: whistling, learning, singing, sleeping in sleeping bags, selling Bibles, sharing street meetings, praying, and playing. Rocky now tries to make quality time for his own children.

Be careful that you're not too busy with other things because you don't know how to cope with your child. This special person emerging from the cocoon of babyhood is becoming a person you may not always quite understand. But he is part of you. God entrusted him to you for nurturing and training. If you lack wisdom, ask of God.

Whenever I have spoken on the subject of faith in the home, I have read a letter that our daughter Mona Ré wrote to us on her 28th birthday. This letter says to us as parents that it's worth it, it can be done, and our children will rise up to call us "blessed." I'll share the letter with you:

My very beloved mommy and daddy,

The house is asleep and I was thanking the Lord for a wonderful year, and high on my list were two wonderful parents. I'm so glad I was able to be with you both this summer in Springfield for a few days, and with Mommy here this fall. They were highlights in my year.

How can I thank God enough for allowing me to grow up in your home? I have been exposed to two special individuals who were not only physical parents, but also spiritual teachers and priests, and prayer warriors. True examples of love, and of how rich a life can be if it is lived unselfishly for others. You've not only told me, but also "shown" me what real life is all about.

Thank you for your love,
for the thousands of tears and prayers,
for making God's work appealing,
for trusting me enough to make my own decisions,
for the costly art lessons,
for the many trips to the dentist,
for the love of flowers and pretty things,
for running with me at 5:00 a.m.,

for loving my friends,
for the family trip to Europe,
for the many letters,
for memories of "Charlies," operas, and the curtain-shop restaurant,
for a room of my own and good books,
for special birthday parties with apple bobbing and "squash pie,"
for a beautiful wedding,
for ice cream breaks at ISUM where I studied with Daddy,
for listening to music over a steak and salad,
for being at the youth "campamentos,"
for the love of a good bargain,
for correcting my term papers,
for loving my husband,
for the feeling of self-worth,
for the knowledge of truth.

I love you, I love you, and I thank you—for everything. I'll be forever indebted to you, but most of all to my Lord.

Tenderly, your 28-year-old,
but still your little,
Mona Ré

Sharing Time

1. What do you talk about in the car? Be aware of your conversation the next time, and write it down. Is it God-honoring?

2. What is the first thing you say when your children return from school? Does it make them want to come home?

3. Do your neighbors know you are a Christian? How can they tell?

4. When you go on vacation, do you forget about attending church?

5. Do you compliment your child? (Proverbs 25:11).

6. Are you afraid to thank your child?

7. Do you teach your children to say "thank you" and "pardon me"? Do they excuse themselves from the table?

8. What kind of prayer do you pray at the table?

9. What kind of pictures or posters do your children have in their rooms? Are they all of football heroes, rock singers, movie stars, and characters like Snoopy? What do these expressions of interest say about their present priorities? about yours?

10. What kind of books and magazines do you have in your home?

11. What kind of magazines do you have in your bathroom? This "rest stop" may be the only place they'll take time to read. Even here we can be training our family. Plant good magazines such as *Woman's Touch, Pentecostal Evangel, Guideposts,* and *Christian Herald.*

7

Working Together in Discipline

"Rocky, do you want to take a walk with me?" My husband spoke to our 6-year-old who was being rebellious at the table. Two-year-old Rachel answered, "Oh yes, Daddy, I'd love to take a walk with you!" That wasn't exactly what Monroe had meant. Rocky scowled defiantly, so Monroe took his hand and led him away from the table to the bedroom. I could hear the discussion, and then the spanking.

It made me feel bad. Rocky was intelligent and had a kind heart, but he had also inherited a streak of stubbornness from both sides of the family. My food tasted a little like cardboard, but I tried to smile and continue eating. It was important not to allow this discipline session to upset the whole family. Life must go on.

The discipline also went on. We heard Monroe ask, "Now are you going to obey?" Apparently Rocky shook his head "no." More spanking. "Now are you going to obey?" There was more spanking, so the answer must have once again been "no." More spanking. Finally we heard the sobs. "Yes, Daddy. Yes, Daddy. Yes, Daddy."

His daddy pulled him into his arms to love him. "Rocky, we love you. That is why we must discipline you, although it hurts us to do it." He held him tight, and wiped away the tears. Then they both returned to the table. I don't think we ever had to spank Rocky again. From that day on we could talk with him and he would listen; he was obedient. He had a tender heart. But it had been necessary for him to learn who the authority was in the home. To conquer the will without crushing a child's spirit is very important.

The Mother's Attitude

It was important for me to be supportive of my husband's disciplinary action. Parents may disagree to a certain extent, but they should never let the child know this. They should avoid anything that would undercut the authority of the disciplining parent. If there is any discussion about how to discipline, it should be held in private away from the children. If the mother has disciplined during the day (and I certainly don't think the father should be the ogre who is always used as a threat: "Wait till your father gets home, then you'll catch it!") the father mustn't lend an ear to tattling in the evening. If the child says, "Mommy spanked me today!" the father must assume that it was for the child's good. There will be time enough later for the parents to discuss what happened.

Some Disagree

I heard a psychologist say, "You mustn't ever *hit* a child. When you tell your child you love him and then hit him, you are developing the battered child, battered wife, abused parent, and fractured home syndrome." However, I believe there is a difference

66

between hitting and spanking. I don't believe you should ever *hit* a child impulsively or at random, but God has provided a nice padded cushion that is adequate for spanking.

I also believe you shouldn't use your hand in spanking. The hand is part of you, so don't offend your child with your person. You might use a little switch or a limber paddle. These will sting without bruising. In fact, you will soon notice that a child will develop a real respect for that paddle. The hand should be reserved for touching, showing tenderness, stroking, ruffling the hair, and patting the shoulders.

Visiting

Our grandson Nathan has his father's middle name, Vaughn, and also his father's spunk. My grandmotherly heart went out to the little fellow when I saw Rocky get down a small, lightweight Ping-Pong paddle. "No, Daddy, no, I'll be good," Nathan promised.

Don't you mix in this, Grandma. The training and disciplining of children is one of the most delicate things God has entrusted into parents' hands.

This is why the Word says in Colossians 3:21: "Fathers, provoke not your children to anger, lest they be discouraged." God knew we needed that word. Ephesians 6:4 also says: "Provoke not your children to wrath: but bring them up in the nurture and admonition of the Lord."

Here is the real work of discipline. It is not just threats like, "You do that once more, and I'll let you have it!" Threats will create a sour, bitter attitude. It is always better to discipline firmly in love and counsel.

Bringing up Children

I believe nurturing includes bending the will early, so you can reason with the child. At the same time, the mother needs to carefully govern her own spirit and attitudes, for children watch their parents closely. If they can see self-discipline, maturity, and peace in their parents' lives, they will respond and become complete, disciplined individuals themselves. Proverbs 14:29 says: "He that is slow to wrath is of great understanding."

Some "Nevers"

Never strike a child in the face. You might injure an eye or cause a bloody nose.

Never box a child on the ears. You might break the tympanum of the middle ear, making him deaf.

Never strike a child in anger.

Never hit a child with a club.

Never kick a child.

Never scream at your child. Learn to modulate your voice.

Never offend your child's dignity. Spank him in private.

Never withhold going to church or Sunday school as punishment.

Never vent your own emotions on a child. Keep calm—discipline is a discipline.

Many parents shout at their children, and eventually the child quits listening. Shouting is not an effective way to discipline. It may provide a neurotic form of release for the frustrated parent, but what of the child? What happens when he learns to tune out the noise? Lower your voice and whisper! You'll be surprised that your child will actually look at you and listen. He may even think you're sick!

The story is told of a teenager whose first job was to stock vegetables in a supermarket. During his first day on the job he spilled some water. The manager told him to wipe it up, but just then some friends walked in and distracted him. At the end of the day the manager fired him. His mother came in to ask why. The man explained that he had asked the boy three times to wipe up the water, but he had never done it. So the mother asked, "Did you scream at him?" The boy had been conditioned to listen only to a certain pitch and intensity in his mother's voice.

Occasionally I have been in a church where young children are allowed freedom of movement during the service. They wander up and down the aisles, and sometimes even up to the platform. This is distracting and unnecessary. Children can learn at an early age to sit when the occasion calls for it. You may have to bring some extra little things with you to church—a piece of paper and a crayon, a book, a puzzle, or a cracker. A child's attention span is not very long. But he/she can learn to go to church, sit, sing the choruses and songs, and listen to the minister. Participating helps to develop his spiritual awareness and social interaction, and even his vocabulary.

Pray With Them

When we discipline our child we should also pray with him. Once I spanked Rachel Jo for complaining she was the only one of our children who ever had to do anything. She cried, but then we knelt together by the bed and talked to the Lord about it. He drew us together and helped both of us that day. The Holy Spirit is gentle. He can speak to a child's heart and break down the resistance. And He can also remind a mother that she, too, is still learning.

Don't be too proud to admit you have made a mistake by being too harsh or too quick with judgment. Maybe you spanked the wrong child because you listened when someone tattled. Go and ask forgiveness of the child who has been wronged. Be specific concerning where you were wrong. This child of yours is a person you are bringing up in your home. He is a whole person who has dignity, emotions, feelings, and rights. Be firm, fair, and friendly in your dealings.

Dr. Kenneth Gangel, in his book *The Family First* (Winona Lake, IN: BMH Books), says discipline is more than punishment. Punishment is the inflicting of hurt for the elimination of undesirable behavior, but discipline is the reinforcement of desirable behavior. It is actually establishing boundaries or fences, or drawing the line, so the child understands the boundaries. Punishment comes when the child breaks through the fence or crosses the boundary line.

Discipline must be consistent and applied in a rational rather than emotional state. If you tell a child "no," then yield after he throws a temper tantrum, you are reinforcing his unacceptable behavior. You are teaching that tantrums are the way to get what you want. Discipline leads the child from dependence on his parents to independence; from following parental guidance to being able to make his own decisions.

Let's Go to the Word

Why Discipline?

1. Proverbs 13:24—to show love, not hate
2. Hebrews 12:1-11—example of God; we are sons
3. Proverbs 3:11,12—God corrects out of love
4. Proverbs 29:15—rod and reproof give wisdom
5. Proverbs 19:18—chasten while there is hope
6. Proverbs 22:15—foolishness in the heart of the child
7. Ecclesiastes 8:11—heart is evil; correct quickly

Positive Effects of Discipline

1. Proverbs 29:17—rest for your soul; fulfillment of responsibility
2. Proverbs 22:6—direction
3. Proverbs 23:13,14—deliverance
4. Proverbs 23:15—joy

My husband's old German father used to say, "Any fool can father a child, but it takes a real man to train him."

Once again we return to God's promise to us: "If any of you lack wisdom, let him ask of God, that giveth to all men liberally, and upbraideth not" (James 1:5). God doesn't scold us when we make a mistake. He doesn't sneer at us; He helps us. Pray about the delicate matter of discipline for each child in your home.

Sharing Time

1. Remembering that discipline is more than punishment, think of ways you might reward and reinforce acceptable behavior. You might like to

71

make a wall chart for your child's room, giving points for each day's activities: brush teeth; make bed; read the Bible; pick up clothes. Promise an outing or some other reward for a certain number of points.

2. Talk over some facet of this chapter with your child to explain why discipline is necessary. Discuss with your spouse the methods and effects of the discipline used in your home.

3. Read some of the portions of Scripture mentioned in this chapter with your children. How do they feel about what God says?

4. What are some of the methods of reinforcement or discipline other parents you know have used? Discuss these ideas, always remembering the uniqueness of each child.

5. Watch your child "discipline" her doll. You'll see a picture of yourself.

8

Coping With Outside Influences

My friend remarked, "Betty Jane, your lawn is full of creeping charley! It's coming right under the fence from your neighbors. It will soon flower and ruin your yard!"

I had gone to my yard every morning, but I went to look at the roses! So now I took another look, and there it was—a dark purple plague running close to the ground. I called the lawn spraying service and the man said, "Not even spraying kills creeping charley. You have to get down on your hands and knees and pull it out!"

There was a lesson in this. I hadn't noticed the voracious weed crawling under the fence and choking my lawn. But I did hear the shouting of venom and hatred that often came spilling over the top of the fence:

"You demon!"

"I'll beat your head in!"

"You devil! Why are you doing that?"

These expressions offend my ears, hurt my heart, and injure my psyche. While I was enjoying my roses, those undesirable influences were probably entering the hearts and attitudes of the children nearby. While the purple plague spread along the ground, another more sinister plague was attacking young lives! Some of my neighbors say they have no idea where their children learn the words they use. The children often don't understand the significance or shades of meaning in the words. They are simply repeating what they have heard. The only way to heal this plague is to get down on our knees. We must ask God to keep our children from contamination, and to give us wisdom to lead our neighbors to Jesus.

In one neighborhood where we lived, we knew the moment our neighbors returned home. Our peace was shattered by complaints, whines, screams, and shouts from the other side of the fence. In fact, when tragedy struck one of our neighbors we weren't alarmed by the shouting because we were used to it!

The Spirit of the Age

My mother used to say, "We must beware of the spirit of the age. It can rob us of the brooding of the Holy Spirit in our lives." We see a vivid picture of the "spirit of the age" in *The Living Bible*'s rendition of 2 Timothy 3:1-5:

> You may as well know this too, Timothy, that in the last days it is going to be very difficult to be a Christian. For people will love only themselves and their money; they will be proud and boastful, sneering at God, disobedient to their parents, ungrateful to them, and thoroughly bad. They will be hardheaded and never give in to others; they will be constant liars and troublemakers and will think nothing of immorality. They will be rough and cruel, and sneer at those who try to be good. They will betray their friends; they will be hotheaded, puffed up with pride, and prefer good times to worshiping God. They will go to church, yes, but they won't really believe anything they hear. Don't be taken in by people like that.

74

But there is an antidote to these evils of which Paul wrote 2,000 years ago.

Dedicate Your Baby

As soon as you know that you are going to have a child, surround and bathe that baby with prayer. Pray everyday that God's Spirit will uphold and protect the child. Psalm 139:13-17 tells us we are known by God in the womb before we are born.

As soon as possible after the baby comes, dedicate him to the Lord. Come to your minister with the baby in your arms, and stand before the congregation as you vow to teach, guide, shelter, love, and pray for that child.

Our newest grandchild was born early on Good Friday morning, so Mona and Mike named her April Dawn. Eight days later it was our privilege to be with them as they dedicated the baby to the Lord. We need this public act which implores God to guard our child from sickness and evil, and acknowledges our need for wisdom to train and bring him up in the right way. God honors this act.

I was talking with a couple whose children are all serving God. I asked, "What is your secret?"

They responded, "We dedicated them to the Lord as early as possible. We found this to be a keeping element. The children knew where the guidelines were, so they were never rebellious."

Children want to know who has the authority. This is the secret. A leading educator said the problem with children today is they don't know who actually has the authority. Is it the school? Some parents undercut any decision the teacher makes and show disdain for the school's authority. Do the parents have the authority? Some teachers call them "old fogeys" and suggest that young people may choose an alternative life-style. Thus, many teachers are undercutting the sanctity of marriage and a godly home. Some propose homosexuality as an alternate life-style. Who holds the authority? Is it the pastor? Unfortunately, many homes have "roast preacher" for Sunday dinner, so the children lose their respect for him.

Back to the Word

Let's read 2 Timothy 3:14,15:

> But you must keep on believing the things you have been taught. You know they are true, for you know you can trust those of us who have taught you. You know how, when you were a small child, you were taught the holy Scriptures; and it is these that make you wise to accept God's salvation by trusting in Christ Jesus (*The Living Bible*).

Timothy's father was a gentile, but his mother and grandmother were godly women of faith. They had instilled in him the Word of God, so he didn't suffer the effects of coming from a divided home. The Word kept him.

Television's Influence

Some polls tell us that preschool children watch an average of 33 hours of television a week, and that 17 percent of our population in 1979 was preschoolers. People have made the television set the baby sitter, the security blanket, and the educator. That takes the responsibility off the parent. "Go sit down with your tray by the TV, Johnnie. Then you'll be quiet."

A group of boys was asked, if they had to choose between having their father or the television set, which would they choose? Ninety-two percent preferred the TV.

It has been reported that 75 percent of the people who write programs slanted to children are influenced by the occult. If you sit down and watch Saturday morning television, you may see that your child is already being programmed to accept magic. This is a subtle trick of the enemy to infiltrate the lives of our children.

A 12-year-old boy beat his elderly neighbor to death. She was an old woman who had befriended him. The court concluded that he had watched so much TV that he didn't know the difference between right and wrong! He had spent 8 hours a day watching television. Most of the programs he had viewed were violent. We need to be aware of what our children are watching, and we should monitor the types of programs they see and the amount of time they spend in front of the TV set.

Touching

We live in a day of dilemmas. We hear about children who feel lonely and rejected because no one is close to them; no one touches them at home. Children who are locked in rooms, isolated, and left as animals, will not learn to love. Americans too often seem to be afraid of touching. Even within our churches there is sometimes a lack of warmth. Psychologists are studying this aberration and proposing courses such as "Sensitivity Training." In such courses, people touch, explore, and create intimacy on an artificial, technical level which does not stem from true emotions and feelings.

Henry Fonda, at 75 years of age, said, "I love my children, but in my whole life I couldn't bring myself to say, 'I love you,' to any of them." This is the experience of many.

Men have been taught not to show their emotions. They are told, "Be strong. Don't cry. Don't be weak. Don't show your feelings." Often fathers are out of touch with their children. So, when their children become adults, some fathers find it difficult to express their affection for them. Children need to know they are loved, and touching is an important means of communicating love and caring. This normal expression of affection will keep children from looking outside their home for expressions of tenderness and caring.

We need to reach out and touch people just as Jesus did. As He touched them, they were made whole. We can bring wholeness to wounded hearts by reaching out in love and compassion.

On the other hand, we are becoming aware of the increased number of incidents of sexual abuse of children within the home—by a parent, stepparent, grandparent, sibling, or other relative.

According to a study by Paul Gebhardt and associates at the Indiana University in Bloomington, almost 9 million people in the United States "have experienced incest" (Lorna and Philip Sarrel, "Incest, Why It Is Our Last Taboo," *Redbook*, November 1980).

Here is our dilemma: How can we teach people to touch and to receive the warmth of being loved and touched, and yet guard against the sexual abuse of children?

Once more the Holy Spirit comes to our aid. As we allow the Lord to rule our lives, the Holy Spirit fulfills and satisfies us emotionally. He also alerts us to problem situations and gives us wisdom.

I believe that one of the key words in child rearing is *awareness*. We should know where our children are, who they are with, and what they are doing. If we as women are aware and concerned, we will build a bridge of trust and keep the confidence of our children. We must be able to shelter them and correct the situation if there is any indication of molestation or abuse.

Many girls have come to me after a teaching session and told me about the burden of guilt and rejection they bear because their father abused them as children. Often the incident has been covered up for years. You might say, "It can't happen here." But there was a case of incest even in the tongues-speaking Corinthian church; that is why Paul wrote special instructions to them (1 Corinthians 5). We must be alert and not stick our heads in the sand.

Prostitution

Another problem today is the bustling business of teen prostitution. You can read about it in many newspapers. Most teenage prostitutes, both boys and girls, come from broken families. But sometimes they are young people from churches, who have been deceived into thinking they'll make a lot of easy money and have a luxurious life.

A United Press story about a 17-year-old prostitute described her as having a bright red heel-shaped scar on her chin from one beating, and blisters on her back from another beating with a coat hanger. An ulcer, high blood pressure, and bronchitis, from standing in subzero temperatures, also plagued her. The article continued: "She strolls

New York's streets every night picking up $10 or $20 dates with middle-aged men she calls creeps. She's had every known social disease, performed every sex act. She looks 27."

Many girls have been raped, abused, or otherwise mistreated at an early age. There are franchises that grab these girls to make money off them in the human "meat market." We must give our young people good sex instruction in a healthy setting and help guard them against being deceived. There are excellent books written from a Christian perspective that will be helpful in this area. (See Bibliography.)

Mind Control

The film *Heavenly Deception,* about a young man who became involved with the Unification Church (Moonies), would be good for every parent to see. It shows some of the techniques used to recruit young people. Various cults use mind-controlling techniques that can change bright, open young people into muted robots. These techniques have a deteriorating effect on the body, mind, soul, and spirit of the young people. They promote distrust of parents and promise a "new complete family" that can really be trusted.

Let's look again at 2 Timothy 3:1-5 in *The Living Bible* and note some of the words Paul uses:

> They will be *proud* and *boastful, sneering* at God, *disobedient* to their parents, *ungrateful* to them, and thoroughly *bad.* They will be *hard-headed* and ... constant *liars* and *troublemakers* and will think nothing of *immorality.* They will be *rough* and *cruel,* and *sneer* at those who try to be good. They will *betray* their friends; they will be *hotheaded, puffed up* with pride, and prefer good times to worshiping God.

Have you observed these characteristics? I heard a very young girl say she sued her parents because they wouldn't let her make her own decisions. The court ruled in her favor and sent her to a foster home.

Dr. Spock's theory of giving a child complete self-expression has been one of the most deteriorating influences on the Christian family. Let's ask God for wisdom to lovingly guide our children without "suffocating" them. And, most important, let's train our children in the Word of God.

Sharing Time

1. Clip articles about children's problems (such as child abuse, drugs, abortion, etc.) from periodicals and discuss them.

2. How can we be aware of these problems in our own community and help to solve them?

3. If you find that someone has been abusing your child, what should you do?

4. How can we govern the television programs our child watches?

5. How does one parent handle the situation if the spouse allows the children to watch unsuitable TV programs?

6. Read 2 Timothy 3:1-7. How does this passage relate to Titus 2? Note especially Titus 2:12.

7. Think of a TV program you can watch together and learn from as a family. Are there objectionable TV programs shown in your community at an hour when children are watching? Discuss ways that Christians can encourage local stations toward better programming.

9

Praying for Our Children

A friend of mine called to ask prayer for her 19-year-old son who was in trouble.

We do need to pray when our children are in trouble, but our prayers should start before the child is born. We should surround the unborn life with prayer, then continue praying after the baby's birth.

I have a warm memory of hearing my daddy call my name in prayer. He prayed for each of us six children during the family's evening prayer time. I also remember coming home from school, bounding through the door, and calling, "Mother." If she wasn't baking bread or filling the house with the aroma of her wonderful cooking, I would find her praying in a little basement room near the water heater, where it was warm. She would wipe her eyes with her apron and greet me. I knew she had named each of us in prayer, and now it was togetherness time.

On Saturdays, we sat together near the bedroom window and read the Sunday school lesson from Mother's big leather Bible. Then at the table Daddy would apply the lesson to life and we'd talk about how to live.

It's work to pray. Sometimes we may just say

hollow words to fill the prayer time. But it takes work to really pray, to care, and to share the burden, the grief, the heartache, the anxiety, and the perplexities of living in today's world.

Once while we were living in Argentina, the postman brought an airmail letter from a friend. I ripped open the envelope and began to read it. My legs became weak and I sat down on the patio, as I read the letter in disbelief. The son of a close minister friend had been killed in a tragic shooting. Upon being stopped by the police, the young man had grabbed his gun from the car seat. In the ensuing scuffle, the gun had gone off, killing the boy. The police later found stolen articles in his car and drugs in his apartment. *What had gone wrong?* I wondered. My heart ached for the boy's family.

In Chile, a pastor's wife tearfully confided that she feared she might never again see her son alive. He was a drug addict; and, even though he had been through a rehabilitation program, he was once again stealing to support his habit.

So many outside influences affect our children today. We need to faithfully follow the Lord and to pray daily for our children.

You Hold Their Lifeline

Weep over your children and pray that God will protect their minds, their attitudes, their ideals, and their faith. Mother, lie before the altar of God in prayer, so your child will not lie in the street with the hippies, the "pot" smokers, and those who loosely give up their virginity. There is so much peer pressure today, but your prayers can build a hedge around your child.

One girl confided to her pastor, "I'm pregnant. They made fun of me at school because I was a virgin, so I gave in. Now what?"

Many are facing this situation today. In fact, in some schools it is actually a status symbol to be pregnant. The girls ask each other if they are pregnant *yet*. Both parents and pastors must build a hedge of faith around their young people through prayer and teaching. No one is immune.

Walking along a California seawall with some friends, I saw the hippies, the castoffs, and the spaced-out young people with their weird clothes, unkempt hair, and vacant, faraway stares. I looked into their empty faces, and my heart went out to them. Here was somebody's daughter; some mother's son. Some homes somewhere had had vacant beds for many months.

On a huge green garbage can nearby, a cynic had scrawled, "For the dead bodies." It could have been the truth. I breathed a prayer. What kind of love could draw these lost young people back to their homes?

A Hedge

I love the thought that Job got up every day and prayed for his family. He was the priest, the intercessor. His prayers kept them. In Job 1:10, Satan himself gives a testimony to the effectiveness of God's hedge around Job: "You have built a hedge around him. I can't get to him with my darts!"

We can build a hedge of prayer and faith around our child. We don't have to spoil him to let him know we love him. When was the last time you put your arms around your child and prayed with him? We should pray *with* our children as well as *for* them.

Each morning as we left for school, I heard my mother pray, "I plead the Blood. I apply the blood of the Lamb to the doorpost of this home today." It was a daily covering of God's protection. We lived a hedged-in life.

Parents on Trial

There are young people who could have been saved and rescued if their parents had been wise in living, loving, training, and praying.

In 2 Timothy 1:6, Paul tells Timothy to stir up the gift within him that he had received when Paul placed his hands on him. The laying on of hands is scriptural. We need to touch our children and stand behind them in prayer, not to hover over or suffocate them, but to be there. They need this security. They need to know we are praying.

Time to Pray

We left Rocky in the States to attend college when he was 17 years old, and we returned to Argentina. During the years we were separated, I had an appointment with God each morning. I would awaken, and lift my head just enough to look at the illuminated dial of the clock. It was 4 a.m.—time to pray.

I lifted my heart to the Throne every morning, naming each child, "Rocky, Mona, Rachel," and committing them to God's keeping. Sometimes as I awakened, my heart would be heavy with a burden. Then I knew it was especially important that I pray for God's protection over them during the day's temptations and decisions.

Arise, wake up. Sometimes we are so busy with our committee meetings, prayer circles, women's meetings, or men's breakfasts, that we don't have time for that child in our home. Even at church we take the time to stop and speak to someone; with no thought for our own children. There are our young people under conviction, but the moment is easily lost while their parents are chatting.

In many services we've seen young people stream to the altar. God is still speaking personally to young people. The Holy Spirit still does His work. But we as parents need to be aware of the moving of God and be there praying *with* our children.

I like to see families sit together in church, but sometimes the church's programs scatter us rather than unite us. Perhaps pastors should declare at least one Sunday a month as "family Sunday," and encourage children to sit with their parents. Then we would see who belongs to what family, and the experience of worshiping and learning together could strengthen family ties.

It is heartwarming to see families sitting together, sharing a hymnbook, praying together, and partaking of Communion together. Pray *with* and *for* your children. It will heal their hearts, and melt any bitterness.

In Lew Wallace's novel, *Ben Hur,* Ben Hur says, after seeing Jesus die on the cross, "I felt His voice draw the sword out of my hand." This is the effect our prayers will have on our children.

The picture in the Book of Lamentations of the children being destroyed is tragic:

I have cried until the tears no longer come; my heart is broken, my spirit poured out, as I see what has happened to my people; little children and tiny babies are fainting and dying in the streets (Lamentations 2:11, *The Living Bible*).

Babies that had once been swaddled and hugged by their mothers were being devoured by the enemy.... And it happens today as it happened then.

Your Profit?

I have paraphrased Mark 8:36 to say: "For what shall it profit a man, if he shall gain the whole world and lose his own son?" Families who pray together stay together.

No home is immune from evil today. We must pray together with our children to guard them.

I sing this prayer song to myself each day, as I think about my children ministering in their respective areas. And I offer it as I send my husband off on an airplane for another month of overseas teaching.

The Prayer Perfect

> *Dear Lord, kind Lord,*
> *Gracious Lord, I pray,*
> *Thou wilt look on all I love*
> *Tenderly today.*
> *Weed their hearts of weariness,*
> *Scatter every care.*
> *Down the wake of angel wings*
>   *winnowing the air.*
> *Bring unto the sorrowing*
> *All release from pain;*

Let their lips with laughter
Overflow again;
And with all the needy, Oh, divide,
I pray, This vast treasure of content
That is mine today!

James Whitcomb Riley

Sharing Time

Discuss some of the needs of your children. Take time to pray together.

88

10

Leading Our Children to God

How early can a child learn to pray?

Some say, "Don't clutter their lives until they enter the accountability stage." But prayer should be as natural as breathing for a child.

When I was 8 years old, my mother had all of us children gather around my father's bed. He was very sick with a gall bladder attack. She called the minister and he anointed my father with oil, and we all knelt and prayed together in faith. God met his need and my father lived to age 87. James 5:15 says: "The prayer of faith shall save the sick, and the Lord shall raise him up." Faith grows in the life of a child.

Let's Pray

Our three children grew up during the years of the revolution in Bolivia, South America. At night we could hear the machine guns and feel the explosions rock our house. The children would come running into our bedroom, calling, "Mommy! Daddy! They're shooting; let's pray!" Then things would quiet down and the children would fall asleep. But when the noise started again, they would run back to our bedroom and ask, "Doesn't God hear us when we pray?"

What could we say? "Yes, God hears, and He watches over us even in the midst of the problem. We can go back to sleep." Children can learn early that God keeps us.

Children need to learn personal prayers. They need to learn to pray for daily help and protection, and to pray when they go to bed, at mealtime, before school, and during family devotions.

Prayer mustn't be used as a whip. "Now you be quiet; we're going to pray."

My husband and I taught a seminar in Argentina, where Rocky directed a Bible school, and we were able to spend some time in Rocky's home. At the time, his son Nathan was 2½ years old. At each meal Nathan would say, "I'll pray, Daddy." And he would pray for Mommy, Daddy, Larisa, Grandma and Grandpa, and his uncles and aunts. Then he would add, "And, Lord, for the food too." I tried to help him remember to pray in Jesus' name.

Children need to be taught how to pray, but they can also learn from hearing us pray. They can talk to God right out of their hearts. It isn't necessary for them to use "thees" and "thous" and flowery words.

When Mona and Mike were missionaries in Spain, Kristi was 3 years old. One day, Mike looked up and exclaimed, "Bless the Lord!" Kristi finished it with, "All my sores!" She didn't understand the word *soul*, but she knew what sores were!

"Et Cetera"

One time in Bolivia when Rocky was about 8 years old, I heard him praying, "Now, Lord, You know all the things I can't remember, the ones I've forgotten. Just take care of it all, *et cetera.*"

90

I said, "Rocky, where did you learn to pray like that?"

"Well, I heard one of my uncles pray that way for things he couldn't remember."

"No, son, God gives us a mind to use and to be specific about the persons we wish Him to bless. God has given us intelligence, and He wants us to tell Him about the situation we need help with. He wants us to use an intelligent approach."

The Special Child

Some children are handicapped—through a birth defect, an injury, a genetic aberration, or some other problem. These children can also learn to pray, and God teaches us special lessons through their membership in our families. We have seen special children pray, intercede, and touch God's throne.

I asked a friend to share with us about the special child God had sent to her home. She told us: "Thirty-six years ago this seemed like an insurmountable hurdle to a young preacher and his wife, but it's turned out to be a blessing in our lives."

She listed four specifics for living with and helping special children:

1. *Accept them.* Nothing can be accomplished in the family relationship or in other situations unless they are accepted. I have seen the downcast look on the face of a special child when he has held out his hand and someone refused to shake hands with him.

2. *Make room for them.* They need a little extra time, care, and patience.

3. *Love them.* They have so much love to give in return.

4. *Give them a chance to learn.* Enroll them early in a school for special children where they can learn as much as possible of the basics. This will give them confidence. Help them to reach their maximum potential.

You Taught Me to Pray

We're told a child learns half of what he will know by the time he's 3 years old. Therefore, teaching a child to pray and have faith is important during those early years. We dare not leave all this training to the Sunday school teacher who has the child for so brief a time each week. It is our responsibility.

On the birthday card Rocky sent us recently from Argentina, he had written: "Thank you for the prayer times. For the memory of kneeling by your bed as I accepted Jesus as my Saviour."

Rachel was 6 when she received the baptism in the Holy Spirit at a South Dakota camp. Then, she expressed a desire to be baptized in water before we returned to South America. A wise pastor filled the baptistry tank at Thanksgiving time for one little 6-year-old girl. Responding to a child's spiritual impulses is important. To cooperate with the spiritual longing in the heart of a child is worth the effort.

As we teach our children to pray, we will realize that the Holy Spirit himself becomes their friend, and God begins to speak to them as their Father. How the child transfers his obedience from his parents to God is a mystery, but it is a wonderful day when we realize our children are hearing *God's* voice and obeying *Him*. Samuel is an example of this. Hannah had kept her promise and given Samuel back to God, and he learned obedience as he served Eli in the temple. When Samuel heard a voice calling him during the night, he answered, "Here am I." Finally he realized it was God speaking to him and he answered, "Yes, Lord, I'm listening." (See 1 Samuel 3.)

Here I Am, Lord

I remember when Mona was a senior in high school in Bolivia. The college catalogs arrived from various schools. She had been accepted at the University of Minnesota and promised a scholarship. Mona had artistic talent and had taken art courses. She had been a big help to us in drawing posters and painting scenes, and in layout. Now it was time to pack the trunk and the suitcases and send her back to the States to go to college. We had trained and taught her, and now we were letting her choose.

Before she left, our family took a winding trip around the mountains for a 3-day youth retreat in a jungle area. One night as I was playing the organ at the front of the humble chapel, I saw each of our three children march down the aisle, one after the other, and kneel on the brick floor next to the crooked altar. I saw the tears flow, and I knew God was speaking to them. They had reached the point of saying, "Yes, Lord, here I am."

Not long after this, I saw the catalog arrive from North Central Bible College. Then various other envelopes from the college were delivered, and we heard a special kind of happy singing when Mona made her decision to go to Bible college rather than the university. She had learned to pray and seek God for herself, and she had also learned to listen to Him.

Then Rocky made up his mind not to go to North Central. He had been offered scholarships from various prestigious schools. But late one night, I found him weeping in the prayer room. A friend had just leaned over and told him, "God gave me a word for you, Rocky: 'It is better to fall on the Rock, than that the Rock should fall on you.' " That was his answer. God wanted him to attend North Central. He had applied to another school, and now God was talking to him.

These are the times when we as parents have to stand behind our young people and be quiet—no pecking; no preaching. If we have taught them to pray and to recognize God's voice, we must believe that God is able to direct them. Perhaps the road they take won't be the one your parental heart would have chosen; it may be entirely different. But each child is a unique person with his own dignity before God. If we have taught our children to seek the Lord, we must loosen the apron strings and trust Him to lead them. We must let them spread their wings and soar up high, close to God's sun.

"Buen Encuentro"

I love the story of Eliezer's journey to seek a bride for Isaac (Genesis 24). He had walked many hot, weary miles as he traveled to Abraham's homeland to look for a God-fearing wife for his master's son. When he arrived in the village, he knelt down and asked God to give him "good speed" (24:12). That is an old English word that doesn't mean much to us today. In Spanish, however, it has real meaning. It is translated *buen encuentro* and expresses a wish that every encounter of the day will be a good one and that God's hand will guide us. So, while our children were growing up, we prayed every day, "Give us *buen encuentro.*" Now sometimes in our children's letters they say, "God gave me *buen encuentro* today."

My son-in-law Steve looked at me quizzically when he heard us pray, "Lord, facilitate our day." I explained to him: "Steve, God knows that 'facilitate' is the equivalent of the 'good speed' of Isaac's story. It means, 'Go before us and smooth our way, so we can follow your guidance.' " It is a good prayer; God answers it and smooths the road ahead of us in each situation.

My brother sings this lovely song:

When Children Pray*

*When children pray, all lovely things more lovely
    seem to be,
All beauty grows more beautiful to see.
When children pray, all sweetness grows more
    sweet;
All tenderness alike becomes more deep;
New forces stir and waken from their sleep
When children pray.*

*When children pray, all growing things rejoice,
And life's eternal hymn grows more profound;
When children pray, the voices of all living
    things are hushed;
The world in all humility draws near,
And God within His heav'n bends down to hear,
When children pray.*

---

*"When Children Pray," words and music by Beatrice Fenner. Copyright 1961 by Shattinger-International Music Corp., Miami Beach, Florida. Used by permission.

Instead of our usual "Sharing Time" feature, here is a guide to family devotions prepared by our son Rocky. Read and discuss it together, and decide which ideas will help your family. Some of these suggestions may be helpful as you teach your children to pray.

Family Devotions: A Key to Communication and Fun

Our Goals in Having Family Devotions

1. To put Jesus at the center of the family.
2. To help each family member grow in the knowledge of God and His Word.
3. To help each person learn how to express himself naturally about the Lord.
4. To help each person learn how to pray naturally.
5. To give a sense of "now-ness" to the Christian life and the Bible.
6. To find that being a Christian is interesting, challenging, and even fun.
7. To bring the family together in an atmosphere of peace and acceptance.

Different Devotional Ideas

BIBLE READING:

1. Have different members of the family read.
2. Pantomime Bible stories.
3. Give each person an "Our Daily Bread" card to read to the group and say what it means to him.
4. Read two versions of the Bible at once.
5. Study Bible characters.
6. Do a "family tree" for Jesus' lineage.

7. Match the time of the year with the devotional readings.

PRAYER:

1. Have one person pray for every other family member on a particular night.
2. Form a circle, then have each person pray a sentence prayer.
3. Have each person, from the youngest to the oldest, pray. (But don't use this idea all the time.)
4. Pray conversational prayers.
5. Have each person pray for the one on his right.
6. Intercessory prayer—have each one name a friend and his need.

OTHER IDEAS:

1. Use a daily devotional guide in addition to reading the Scripture passage.
2. Read other challenging, up-to-date Christian books along with the regular Bible passage, and then discuss them. Some good books are: *Crisis Experiences in the Lives of Noted Christians* by Dr. V. Raymond Edman (Minneapolis: Bethany Fellowship, 1970); *How Great Christians Met Christ* by James C. Hefley (Chicago: Moody Press); and *The Pilgrim's Progress* by John Bunyan (available from Gospel Publishing House).
3. Once in a while, have a time of singing and let each one choose a favorite song.
4. Think of a good question for each person to answer. (For example: "When do you feel closest to God?")
5. Listen to a Christian tape together.
6. Have each person think of a question to ask.

COMMUNICATIONS/DEVOTIONS:

1. Have each person answer the question: "What's the most interesting thing that has happened to you within the last 24 hours?"
2. Parents need to make sure no one interrupts the one who is talking, regardless of his age.

THINGS TO REMEMBER:

1. Variety is the spice of life. Don't let family devotions be boring.
2. If you aren't able to take the full 15 minutes for devotions one day, at least pray together every day and save the devotions for the next day. Don't give up on the whole idea just because you've missed 1 or 2 days.

11

Stretching Family Finances

"That is a darling blouse," said my friend. "Where did you get it?"

"At my favorite boutique."

"Really? Which one this time?"

"At the high school flea market. The proceeds will be used to buy new band uniforms."

"I can't believe it! I wish you'd write down some of your secrets to help us. We just don't know how to stretch our finances."

Early Training

I remember Mother sending me to the bakery one block away when I was 4 years old. I was supposed to ask for day-old caraway rye bread. Instead, it came out, "Yesterday's black bread with take-away seeds." So after that it was known as the "take-away seed bread."

Mother showed me how to read the sale ads when I was 7. She taught me how to comparison shop. If oranges were 29¢ a dozen in one store and 49¢ in another, I learned to buy them where they were cheaper. I checked the difference in hamburger prices, and she showed me how to examine the heads of lettuce and pick the ones that were heavier and fresher. I've passed this knowledge on to my girls.

I grew up during the depression years. There were five other children at home, so Mother had to budget carefully. She taught me to buy liver for 15¢ a pound, and to stretch a can of salmon to feed the eight of us by using cream sauce and toasted, day-old bread. I never felt poor. I felt fortunate because I was learning to stretch the grocery money.

One day a neighbor said to me, "Your clothes might be patched, but they're always clean." Yes, and we even had piano lessons. Mother always sent a carefully wrapped package of stiffly-ironed white shirts with me each time I went for my lesson. Later, I realized that my college-educated, teacher mother was paying for my piano lessons by washing and ironing shirts! In today's society you could either say it was beneath her, or she had learned to trade services, since she had more determination than money.

I remember my first recital. One of my aunts had given my mother a blue serge suit. Mother bought a red taffeta remnant on sale, and I went to my recital wearing a blue skirt, a blue cape with a red lining, and a bright red blouse with a big bow. I was the best-dressed girl in the recital because Mother was ingenious.

Good Manners

My aunt would say, "Your grandfather was an aristocrat." To me that meant: You might not have money, but you can still have good manners, good breeding, and dignity. This helped me.

During my high school days, I earned money to pay for my own music lessons by playing the organ at a mortuary. I paid for a concert series ticket by turning pages for the artists, and I got to meet lots of interesting people. I still had time for extra-curricular activities like the band and orchestra, and the drama, radio, and Spanish clubs. I even joined the rifle club. But the bullets cost too much, so I had to drop out. Today's young people need to be given a chance to use their ingenuity to earn their own money—by mowing lawns, running errands, sweeping sidewalks, or shoveling snow.

Garage Sales

During one of our furloughs, someone remarked that several of her friends got together on Friday mornings and made the rounds of the "garage sales." Now that was a new and strange idea to me.

I was busy studying, so I didn't have Friday morning free. Occasionally, however, we began to stop at garage sales on the way home in the afternoon, and I soon learned that delicate art. One year we bought ice skates for $2 instead of $20 a pair. We also bought gloves, jackets, and sweaters for all five of us that would serve until the after-Christmas sales, when we could buy new clothes. We stretched our limited missionary budget many times by having a good eye at garage sales.

Eclectic

I like the new word decorators use, *eclectic.* The dictionary defines eclectic as "selecting what appears to be the best from various sources."

Thinking of our home, I laughed when I heard one interior decorator use that word. Our home is early garage sale and late estate sale! We have furniture from various periods, but it all goes together. We feel comfortable with the way it blends, and also with the fact that it fits our pocketbook. In decorating your home, eclectic covers everything that you really enjoy and can mesh together—as long as it blends.

We called about an ad in a sale sheet, and an old gentleman said, "This chair has been sat in only once and a half!" It was true; the chair was nearly brand-new. And we bought it from him for one-fifth of the price he had paid for it.

Some girls decide they have to have a special piece of furniture or something in a certain color, and they spend time and gas hunting for just that one detail. I married a young minister who was starting out in a pioneer church. Each week we received the Sunday morning offering, which would fluctuate. One week it would be $6.52; another week it would total $11.33—but I learned to make it stretch. Another newly married pastor not far from us insisted on having all new matching furniture. That couple went heavily into debt and eventually left the ministry altogether. I believe God's Word teaches us that contentment is the most important quality in building a happy home and a good marriage.

We've already mentioned that *money* is one of the main factors leading to divorce, so learning how to be thrifty and make the budget stretch is vital. There is a lot of talk nowadays about survival. Throughout the Bible, God gives us His secrets for survival. David said: "I have been young, and now am old; yet have I not seen the righteous forsaken, nor his seed begging bread" (Psalm 37:25). God is for us, but we must be good stewards of what He has entrusted us with.

If you see an excellent buy, work other small details around it. We made our first bookcase out of boards and bricks. A folding table we had purchased at a farm auction served as our desk, and we accented it with a lovely winding philodendron plant. These two pieces of furniture filled one wall of our first home. We also covered a 25-year-old davenport that had been given to us, with a bright, floral, king-size sheet from the sale table. The room was a contentment center.

Unfortunately, many young people today want to start out at the same level on which their parents are living after 25 years of marriage and saving. Sometimes it's the mother of the bride who projects this level of expectancy: "If he can't support you in the manner in which you're accustomed to living. . . ."

Be Thrifty

Being thrifty doesn't mean being stingy or mean, or hoarding for hoarding's sake—just to count how many cans you have. Rather, to be thrifty is to use what you have and exercise caution in buying. Then you will have more to share with others and be able to be hospitable, which is a Christian grace.

One of the best books offering money-saving tips is *How to Save Money on Almost Everything,* by Neil Gallagher (Minneapolis: Bethany Fellowship, 1978). It brings a scriptural slant to buying everything from eggs and vegetables to cars, insurance, and legal expenses.

"Brown Bag It"

Lots of people feel they have to go out to lunch every day. Do you know what this means? There is the extra expense for lunch, plus tips and gas. We have found we save a lot of money by "brown bagging it." We eat a nice tasty lunch that has been prepared with some forethought. I fix extra broiled chicken at night, then save a piece or two in a plastic bag. The next day we enjoy the chicken, along with yogurt and celery, instead of "junk food." Sometimes I roast extra meat and save some for sandwiches. Day-old bread can be bought at bakery outlets and kept frozen until you're ready to use it. Instead of buying expensive cold cuts, a stew or soup made from the previous evening's meal provides a good lunch. Use your ingenuity.

Shopping Tips

Supermarkets often have a shelf for "fast clearance" items. Dented cans can usually be bought at reduced prices and, if they aren't punctured, they are a good buy. I also check the damaged cereal boxes. If the inner wrapping isn't torn, the food is still good. Store coupons may be used for additional savings.

Most delicatessens take the end slices of their cheese or lunch meat, put them in bags, and sell them at a "special price." For young people starting out on a limited income, being thrifty is very important. In this area, I believe that God helps those who help themselves by cutting corners. However, don't buy something just because it's on sale. If you're not going to use it, it's no bargain!

Another way to save money is to turn off any lights that you aren't using. You'll be surprised how much you will save on your electric bills. Make all long-distance phone calls during the low-rate hours. The nighttime rates are considerably less than the daytime rates.

Wastefulness

A young pastor from Korea visited the States for a conference. Upon returning home, his friends asked him what had been the most outstanding thing about his visit. He replied, "The size of the garbage cans!"

Americans throw out 20 percent of their food. In a restaurant, be careful not to order more than you can eat, or ask for a "doggie bag" to take the extra food home. Leftovers can often be used to make a tasty casserole or soup.

In the Lord's Prayer, there is the petition: "Give us this day our daily bread" (Matthew 6:11). I tell my children that God promises to give us our daily bread, and He often puts butter and jam on it too! Our attitude is very important. If we open our hands to help others, God will help us.

Many times we may not have money for entertainment and cultural enjoyment, but our needs can be met in other ways. Take advantage of a free concert in the park, an art display, or a floral design contest. At Christmas you can feast your eyes on the displays that others make, and get ideas from them. Keep your own decorations simple.

Sharing Time

Read and discuss the following Scripture passages:

1. "My God shall supply all your need according to his riches in glory by Christ Jesus" (Philippians 4:19).

2. "The young lions do lack, and suffer hunger: but they that seek the Lord shall not want any good thing" (Psalm 34:10).

3. "Better is a handful with quietness, than both the hands full with travail and vexation of spirit" (Ecclesiastes 4:6).

4. Give to the poor and the needy (see Proverbs 31:20).

5. Scatter, and increase; withhold, and be in poverty (see Proverbs 11:24).

6. Prove God with your tithe. The first 10 percent is not yours; it's God's. He will make the rest stretch. (See Malachi 3:10.)

7. Chapters 8 and 9 of 2 Corinthians are full of the grace of giving, the virtue of being liberal. Go through these two chapters and underline the words *grace, abundant, gift,* and *liberality.* A key verse is 2 Corinthians 9:7: "God loveth a cheerful giver." The churches in Macedonia gave generously, even though they were in deep poverty. The promise is given here that if we will be generous in giving to God's work, and in opening our hearts and homes and ministering to others, God will provide for our needs (v. 8). We give because we love, and God gives back to us by helping us stretch what we have.

8. Memorize Matthew 6:33,34 to help you have the right attitude toward finances: "But seek ye first the kingdom of God, and his righteousness; and all these things shall be added unto you. Take therefore no thought for the morrow."

12

Being a Good Mother-in-Law

"Mommy, I love you. You're really a good sport!" These words are one of my fondest memories. My 6-foot-tall son-in-law said them spontaneously after our family spent an evening sharing games.

Society has done a cruel injustice to mothers-in-law by the ever-present taunts and jokes at their expense. The role of a mother-in-law is a delicate one, and none of us has experience in it before we become one. Once again, we are reminded of James 1:5: "If any of you lack wisdom, let him ask of God." The Lord doesn't scold us if we make a mistake in this new relationship. I would like to change the expression *mother-in-law* to "mother-in-*love*." Possibly our attitudes would change if we changed our terminology.

Multiply Not Subtract

We had two weddings during a 6-week period, and we gained a son and a daughter. These members who are added to our family structure through marriage do not bring the loss of our beloved children; rather, they bring added blessings to our home. They add personality, wit, vitality, and stamina. In fact, they not only add blessings to our home, they also multiply them because there are more people for interacting. We multiply the dimensions of intercommunication with each additional person.

When Monroe and I married, we had two ways of interacting. When our first child was born, we had six. With three children, there were a possible 20 ways. When two of our children married, we had 42 directions of interacting, and when our daughter Rachel brought Steve into our family, there were 56 possible directions of communication.

It Seems So Final!

One of my friends had a crying jag the week after her son's wedding. "It seems so final! It seems like the whole family has changed!" she said. Yes, that is true in one respect. When a son or daughter marries, the family grows larger and must absorb a new and different personality. But the Holy Spirit also helps us to enlarge our attitudes and accept and not reject this "different" person.

Esau took *two* wives when he was 40 years old (Genesis 26:34). (It would seem he was old enough to have known better!) Both girls were Hittites. They were from a pagan culture and had customs that were different from those of Esau's parents. They brought bitterness of spirit to Isaac and Rebekah (26:35). The Targum (an Aramaic translation of the Old Testament) tells us these wives quarreled constantly and rebelled against religious instruction.

Choosing an unsaved partner can cause enmity in the home. Genesis 28:8 tells us Esau realized that his pagan wives didn't please his parents, so to placate Isaac and Rebekah he took two more wives—this time from the family of Ishmael, the son of his grandfather Abraham. This really multiplied the problems. From this Biblical example, we can see the bitterness that can be caused for the mother-in-law when there is contention, strife, and quarreling in the family.

Better Than Seven Sons

The Book of Ruth bears Ruth's name, but her mother-in-law, Naomi, was actually the one who made Ruth's story possible.

After the deaths of Naomi's husband and two sons, she and her daughters-in-law decided to leave the land of Moab and return to Judah, Naomi's homeland. As the three widows walked along the road toward Judah, Naomi began to urge the young women to return to their own people and their own land. Finally, Orpah decided to go back to her family. She kissed her mother-in-law good-bye and returned to her homeland, culture, and religion.

But Ruth looked at Naomi and made this wonderful vow:

> Entreat me not to leave thee, or to return from following after thee: for whither thou goest, I will go; and where thou lodgest, I will lodge: thy people shall be my people, and thy God my God (Ruth 1:16).

What a decision! What had Ruth seen in Naomi that inspired her devotion for her mother-in-law? Naomi's life must have been a wonderful testimony of the true God of Israel for Ruth to decide to accompany her to a faraway land, and to accept her culture and her God. So, the two widows found lodging in the village of Bethlehem, and Ruth went out to get a job to support them.

Naomi gave her good counsel. She instructed Ruth in the ways of her God and her people (Ruth 3:18). Her advice, paraphrased in our language, was: "Be quiet; sit still; be patient. Don't get uptight in your new situation. Don't sweat the small stuff. God guides our paths."

While Ruth worked in Boaz' fields, did she feel sorry for herself? "Poor me! Here I am among these strange people, and I have to work so hard!" No, I don't think so. Her attitude would have been reflected in the quality of her work and on her face.

Boaz was the son of Rahab, the ex-harlot from Jericho. His mother had probably told him about some of the adjustments she had had to make and what it had been like to learn the culture and customs of a new people. So, Boaz was able to understand this girl Ruth and was impressed with the love and kindness she had shown Naomi.

Boaz was a relative of Naomi's husband and an honorable man. Naomi instructed Ruth to ask Boaz to buy their property and marry her, according to the custom of their day. Boaz agreed and became the kinsman redeemer for these two widows. He told Ruth:

> Thank God for a girl like you! . . . For you are being even kinder to Naomi now than before. Naturally you'd prefer a younger man, even though poor. But you have put aside your personal desires (so that you can give Naomi an heir by marrying me) (Ruth 3:10, *The Living Bible*).

The women of the city came to Naomi and blessed her with a great blessing and said: "Thy daughter-in-law, which loveth thee, . . . is better to thee than seven sons" (4:15). They could see that Ruth loved Naomi. In the Jewish culture of that day, a son was more important than a daughter. In fact, Jewish men often prayed, "I thank Thee, Lord, that Thou hast not made me a woman." But the love Ruth and her mother-in-law shared was so great that the women said Ruth was better than seven sons!

When Ruth's baby was born, they named him Obed, which means "serving." Ruth had learned to serve the true God. Naomi took care of the baby and helped raise him. Obed became the grandfather of King David, and was in the lineage of our Lord Jesus Christ. Thus, a Gentile Moabitess was brought into the line of royalty through her devotion to her mother-in-law.

Express Appreciation

I was speaking at some conferences in Costa Rica, while Rocky and Sherry were in language school there, preparing to go to Argentina. Sherry felt pretty disappointed and blue because the doctor had told her she had another month before their new baby would be born. We had been hoping the baby would arrive while I was there to help.

It was their son Nathan's second birthday, so Sherry baked a birthday cake and I fixed Spanish rice. Then we bought a *piñata* in the shape of Donald Duck. It was filled with candy and peanuts, and the next day at the birthday party the children would take turns trying to break it.

During the night, however, Rocky tapped softly on my door and said, "I'm taking Sherry to the clinic. Go ahead with Nathan's birthday party." At

2 o'clock that same morning, Larisa Michelle was born, and we brought Sherry home 2 days later!

I helped take care of Larisa so Sherry could get some rest and continue her language classes. I was reminded of Naomi's example. Sherry and I shared those first days of their baby's life. A tight bond of love developed between us because we shared this special time together.

One of my friends told me: "I received a letter from Sherry and she talks of the love you share. She mentions how much she is learning from you and how you have helped her." This woman was visibly moved to think a daughter-in-law would express such love and appreciation for her mother-in-law.

Often we erect defenses because we feel vulnerable and don't want to get hurt. We feel we're losing our son, so we clam up and remain aloof. Instead, we need to open up and accept our new daughter-in-law so that we can be accepted.

He Will Touch Us

In Matthew 8:14,15, we have a tender picture of Jesus visiting in Peter's home. Peter's mother-in-law, who lived with the family, was "sick of a fever." Usually we think of the apostle Peter as a rugged fisherman, a rough-and-ready outdoor type, who was sanguine, extroverted, and outgoing. But here we see that Peter called Jesus to help his mother-in-law. And Jesus came and touched her hand. Just a gentle touch of Jesus' hand, and she was healed. The fever left her, and she was immediately strengthened. So, she got up and helped serve Jesus and the disciples.

The touch of Jesus not only healed her fever, it

also infused new life into her. Her strength returned, and her vitality and desire to serve were renewed. As women, many times we need the complete well-being that only Jesus' touch can bring us.

Pray Ahead

We need to pray, and to teach our children to pray, for the future marriage partner that God is allowing to grow up somewhere. We should pray that God will keep that one from sin. Then when our children marry, we will feel a kinship has already been established with that son- or daughter-in-law.

The Garbage

We had been ministering in Argentina, and hadn't seen our daughter and son-in-law since their wedding. I had a few things to learn about being a mother-in-law. Mona and Mike lived in a two-bedroom apartment on the third floor. While we were visiting them, I noticed the garbage was starting to accumulate in their apartment. Two enormous, heavy bags stood near the door! My son-in-law walked right around the bags, so I set them closer to the door. But he stepped *over* them. It was a long way down to the first floor!

I was the one who needed to work on my attitudes. I had to learn they'd worked out a different division of work in their home. I prayed for God's help to be quiet. It takes time to work out the kinks in marital adjustments, so we must not expect immediate perfection in the new marriages around us.

Now the garbage at Mona and Mike's house is carried out regularly; it's closer. In Mona's letter which I shared with you in chapter 6, she says:

"Thank you for loving my husband." Love goes a long way. Ask for God to give you His love. Our son-in-law is our son-in-*love*. (Read 1 Thessalonians 4:9.)

Study to Be Quiet

Did you know that 1 Thessalonians 4:11 tells us to "study to be quiet"? If we can be quiet, we can be agents of help and healing in these new relationships. Don't butt in. I heard a mother say, "I'd rather stand at my son's casket than see him marry that girl!"

Maybe we would never make such a remark, but we must be careful not to say things like: "How could you marry that person? His family isn't like us. They are so different!" Such comments simply make our son or daughter more fiercely loyal to the one he or she has chosen, and a chasm begins to develop in our communication and relationship with them. When we make such remarks, we also begin to sow seeds of doubt and discord in their hearts which eventually may become the wedge that drives them apart.

There is a delicate balance. If we do feel a word of counsel is in order, we should speak to each one separately, not while they are together.

Grandchildren

When that handsome young man squares his youthful shoulders and accepts his responsibility as a new father, a change can be seen in him. An authority, an air of responsibility, settles over him like a mantle. His bearing and walk may seem different. Maybe it's the nights of walking the floor and rocking that little one to sleep!

114

Now the "mother-in-love" becomes a grandmother. Once again, there is a delicate line to walk. Can we, as grandparents, love our grandchildren without spoiling them? Can we hug without hurting? Can we avoid creating a shelter for them when their parents want to discipline them? Once again, we must strike a careful balance. We must always defer to the rights of the parents, and love and discipline in such a way that we won't undercut their authority.

Some Dos and Don'ts for Mothers-in-Law

Do	*Don't*
Be patient	Speak sharply
Show appreciation	Complain
Compliment	Undercut
Be loyal	Criticize
Be courteous	Be defensive
Pray for them	Find fault
Include both names when writing	Speak against them
Accept both as your own	Be suspicious
Encourage them	Discourage them

Sharing Time

1. Write a letter to your son- or daughter-in-law, expressing your gratitude that he or she is a part of your family.

2. Think about mother-in-law jokes and make sure they don't apply to you.

3. Try to help your own family and friends realize the cruelty and rejection that a mother-in-law may feel when such jokes are made in public.

4. Could you get along if you lived in the home of Naomi or Peter's mother-in-law? How would *you* have to change?

5. Read Luke 12:53 and Matthew 10:35. What do these passages say about the in-law problem?

6. Do you constantly serve as baby-sitter for your grandchild? How might this interaction with the child undercut the responsibility of your son- or daughter-in-law?

7. If your children aren't married yet, discuss with them the qualities they should look for in a mate.

13

Adjusting to the Empty Nest

We had been choosing clothes for college, lengthening hems, sorting through scrapbooks and special memorabilia, and getting things ready. Now the day had come and it was time to send our last child, Rachel Jo, to college.

Rachel had been born in Bolivia and had graduated from high school in Argentina. She had been my feet during days of sickness and my eyes as we drove through the wild traffic to speak at youth retreats and conferences. When my husband was away teaching, she was my companion. She was my ears at night, and my arms and hands during the day, helping to serve the many guests who came into our missionary home. I would miss her.

Two young Argentine friends accompanied us to the airport to help with the luggage and parking. I was busy checking customs and filling out immigration forms until the moment the plane lifted her away. Then one of the young men said, "She's gone. How does it feel?"

I said, "It feels like not talking."

He wanted me to answer, "God will take care of her." Deep in my heart I knew He would. We had looked forward to this day. We had encouraged her: "You can do it!"

I thought about the time she had contracted hepatitis. She was a junior in high school and missed 5 weeks of classes. After she recovered she was left very weakened from the jaundice, yet she returned to school with a lot of willpower and graduated as valedictorian.

When the college catalogs arrived, we perused them together and thought, chatted, and prayed about the different schools. We sought God's guidance, yet left her free to make her own choice. Her counselor said, "She can write her own ticket; she can be accepted at any school she chooses!"

We knew this happy outgoing blond was a miracle. When she was born her lungs didn't open, and the doctor said it was impossible for her to live—especially at that 13,000-foot altitude. But people prayed with us that night, and she survived. Now our baby, our beautiful Rachel who knew no stranger, was leaving us. . . .

Again my young Argentine friend asked, "How does it feel?"

It was hard to chitchat during the hour-long ride home from the airport, but I did. I needed to show those young people that God gives peace even at such times.

As I walked into our home, I missed Rachel's help with the gates and locks. Her little white bed looked so forlorn; it was smooth and unrumpled now. All the books were in order on her shelves. It was so quiet. So empty.

But we wouldn't have wished it to be different. Since then, I have met other parents who dread the day they will send their child away to college. Yet we mustn't hold our young people back. This is what we have been preparing them for all their lives—to be complete persons with dignity who can walk away bravely and wave good-bye.

God talks to us in His Word about the "empty nest." He reminds us He is our Father. In Jeremiah 31:3, He says: "I have loved thee with an everlasting love: therefore with loving-kindness have I drawn thee." Psalm 91:4 tells us: "He shall cover thee with his feathers, and under his wings shalt thou trust." He is with us even when we are too upset or hurt to talk. God is there; He is a refuge (Deuteronomy 33:27).

Our steps are ordered by the Lord (Psalm 37:23), and our times are in His hands (31:15). God's timing is perfect, so relax! He is "our refuge and strength" (46:1), and He will guide us with His eye (32:8). He is our hiding place and He will preserve us (32:7). The Lord is nigh to the brokenhearted and His ears are open to their cry (34:15,18). None of those who trust in the Lord will be desolate (34:22). God not only hears our cry, He also puts a song in our heart (40:1-5).

Our children need our backing and prayers, not our self-pity. We can create scars and a guilt complex by our attitudes. "Poor me! Here I am all alone—you have deserted me!" Instead, we need to undergird our children so they will be strong and know God in a personal way. We can write to them and remind them of Scripture passages that will keep them during times of loneliness, temptation, and decisionmaking. E. Stanley Jones said, "God has no grandchildren." Our children must know God as their own Heavenly Father.

Reinforce

Our young people need to be reinforced. There is a

certain finality to their leaving. They step out from our home as children, and return from college as mature adults. They think thoughts fashioned by various kinds of teachers, and many different friends enter their lives, but we must relinquish them to God's keeping.

Sometimes I hear parents talk for years in advance about the day their child will leave home, "Boo hoo! Poor me!" They are feeling sorry for themselves and are not creating a trusting climate and a healthy attitude to launch their child into responsible adulthood.

I remember the day in July when we helped Rocky move into the Bible college dormitory. The halls were empty and rang with the sound of our footsteps. We were getting ready to leave for Argentina to continue our teaching ministry among the leaders of Latin America. We had been home just long enough for Rocky to graduate from high school, and now we had to leave him.

He looked like a little yellow canary as he stood at the airport in Minneapolis. We were *leaving him.* Sometimes I think this is harder than for a child to leave home to go away to college, knowing he can return home to visit. He was only 17 and not a very tall young man, but he was a giant inside.

Our steps made a hollow echo as we walked through the tunnel into the airplane. There he stood and waved bravely to us, "Go with God." Then he turned to *stay* and work; to go to college and prepare himself for life.

I turned my face to the window of the airplane, as the hot tears rolled down my cheeks. This wasn't a time to talk. It was just a time to feel, and to *know* that the God who had called us is faithful.

Finish Our Course

The Scripture passage that kept me sane during this time was Acts 20:24: "But none of these things move me, neither count I my life dear unto myself, so that I might finish my course with *joy*, and the ministry, which I have received of the Lord Jesus, to testify the gospel of the grace of God."

God will sanctify your tears. They are therapy. He will bring the balm of Gilead and heal the wounds. He will satisfy the longing of your heart.

I am acquainted with some missionaries who have had to leave their college-age children and return to the mission field. They know God's grace is sufficient and His help is abundant. Someday these young people will do exploits for their God, because their parents have been able to lean on His arms and trust in His love.

Rocky sent us a card with these words written on it: "Thanks for the times of togetherness, the quality times we shared. For laughing, learning, whistling, running, singing, driving, watching, working, praying, and playing." Yes, playing together also reinforces the quality-time memories.

Tough Yet Tender

A woman has to be tough yet tender. She has to be able to take it, to be alone, and yet still be able to feel. As women, we are strong yet fragile. We are the weaker partner, yet at times we must be very strong.

When the mother eagle teaches her young to fly, she carries him up high, then pulls her body away and watches him flutter. For a time she will fly up under him and rescue him, but eventually the day comes when he must fly on his own. Then the mother eagle flies high into the sun and puts some distance between them, as if to say, "Go with God."

We don't want to break a wing; we don't want to cripple our child. We must encourage him to soar, and not let him hear the hollow beating of our heart. Then we must lean on the Lord; He is our refuge and help.

I wonder how Rebekah felt as she watched Jacob trudge off into the night with his pack on his back, some goat's milk cheese, a cornmeal cake, and a bottle of oil? She had been crafty in helping him grasp the blessing that belonged to his older brother Esau. Now he had to leave her. What a help he had been. He liked to cook, and she loved him so much. She loved him *too much!* Could she have known she would never again see this son whom she loved?

When Timothy left with Paul on his missionary assignment, I can imagine that Lois and Eunice had a lump in their throats. The house would be strangely quiet without the young man.

Hannah fulfilled her promise and took Samuel to the temple to live with Eli and learn to minister and serve at the altar of God. Each year she made him a new coat and brought it to him. She could see that Eli's sons were wicked. They were committing fornication with the girls at the temple. She was probably concerned that they would have a bad influence on Samuel, so she undergirded him in prayer.

Biblical mothers felt what we feel. We need to pray, write letters, learn to serve others, and fill our lives with God. He has a work for us to do for Him.

The Critical Stages of a Marriage and Home

Marriage is a process of a lifetime. We must be committed to making our marriage work. There are different stages in a marriage; each with new challenges and opportunities. The following outline lists some of these:

50 Years of Marriage

I. The Couple Alone (2 years or more?)
   A. Get acquainted and build the nest
   B. Learn to know each other—sexually, spiritually, mentally, and emotionally
   C. Cut the umbilical cord and form own home
II. The Birth of the First Child
   A. Share love, life, and work
   B. Be careful of depression, postpartum trauma
   C. Develop and modify roles for shared parenthood (My neighbors have worked this out. The husband said, "Today I'd like to watch the ball game, so I'll fold the diapers." The wife answered, "Great, then I'll mow the lawn.")
   D. Consolidate the partnership and work on communication
III. The Development of the Child(ren)
   A. Teach and discipline the children during this critical time of growth
   B. Help the children grow spiritually
IV. The Marriage of the Child(ren)
   A. "Cut the cord" as each child leaves home
   B. Develop in-law relationships
V. The Couple Alone (the empty nest)
   A. Learn to be a complete couple

The Wheel of Marriage

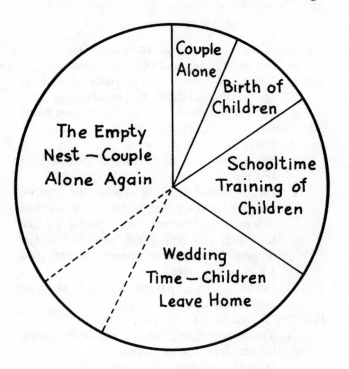

- Couple Alone
- Birth of Children
- Schooltime Training of Children
- Wedding Time — Children Leave Home
- The Empty Nest — Couple Alone Again

B. Don't be slaves of the children
C. Work on communication and take time to talk (Almost half of the couple's married life may be lived without having children at home. A lot of divorces occur at this stage—be careful!)
VI. Special Problems
A. Be gentle in sickness and in health
B. Don't be a "witch" during the menstrual cycle
C. Read about and be aware of the changes that both men and women go through during the middle years (ages 40-60)

Sharing Time

"It takes a heap o' living in a house to make a house a home." And it takes a "heap o' loving" to form a real home out of a marriage. We must determine that "as for me and my house, *we will serve the Lord*" (Joshua 24:15). Ecclesiastes 4:9,10 says that "two are better than one"; if one falls, the other can lift him up.

1. Share an anecdote from your wedding.
2. Share some insights that you have learned. We help each other by being open. Don't think you are the only one who has certain feelings and problems.
3. Pray together for each other. We can help to heal our nation by seeking healing for our own homes, marriages, and families.

Bibliography

Brock, Raymond T. *The Christ-centered Family.* Springfield, MO: Gospel Publishing House, 1977.

Christenson, Larry. *The Christian Family.* Minneapolis: Bethany Fellowship, Inc., 1980.

Conway, Flo, and Siegelman, Jim. *Snapping.* New York: J. B. Lippincott, Co., 1978.

Dobson, James. *Dare to Discipline.* Wheaton, IL: Tyndale House Publishers, 1976.

Fromm, Erich. *The Art of Loving.* New York: Harper & Row Publishers, Inc., 1974.

Gallagher, Neil. *How to Save Money on Almost Everything.* Minneapolis: Bethany Fellowship, Inc., 1978.

Gangel, Kenneth. *The Family First.* Winona Lake, IN: BMH Books.

Grams, Betty Jane. *Women of Grace.* Springfield, MO: Gospel Publishing House, 1978.

L'Abate, Luciano and Bess. *How to Avoid Divorce.* Atlanta: John Knox Press, 1976.

LaHaye, Tim and Beverly. *The Act of Marriage.* Grand Rapids: Zondervan Publishing House, 1976.

Mains, Karen B. *Open Heart, Open Home.* Elgin, IL: David C. Cook Publishing Co., 1976.

Miles, Herbert J. *Sexual Happiness in Marriage.*

Grand Rapids: Zondervan Publishing House, 1967.

Narramore, Clyde M. *Life and Love.* Grand Rapids: Zondervan Publishing House.

Narramore, Clyde M. *Young Only Once.* Grand Rapids: Zondervan Publishing House.

Ortlund, Anne. *The Disciplines of the Beautiful Woman.* Waco, TX: Word, Inc., 1977.

Schaeffer, Edith. *What Is a Family?* Old Tappan, NJ: Fleming H. Revell Co., 1975.

Skoglund, Elizabeth. *Your Troubled Children.* Elgin, IL: David C. Cook Publishing Co., 1975.

Trobisch, Walter C. *I Married You.* New York: Harper & Row Publishers, Inc., 1971.

Wilkerson, David. *The Christian Maturity Manual.* Glendale, CA: Gospel Light/Regal Publications, 1976.

Wright, H. Norman. *Communication: Key to Your Marriage.* Glendale, CA: Gospel Light/Regal Publications, rev. ed. 1979.

Audio Cassettes

Dobson, James. *Focus on the Family Series.* Word, Inc., 4800 W. Waco Drive, Waco, TX 76710 (series of tapes on selected topics. This is different from the film series listed below).

Sproul, T. C. *The Intimate Marriage Series.* The Ligonier Valley Study Center, Stahlstown, PA 15637 (some are in video form also).

Film Series

Dobson, James. *Focus on the Family.* Word, Inc., 4800 W. Waco Drive, Waco, TX 76710 (1979) (used often in seminars).

Heavenly Deception, Evangelical Films, 2848 W. Kingsley, Garland, TX 75041 (80 minutes).

Magazine Articles

Alexander, John and Betty. "Building a Christian Marriage." *HIS* (November 1979): 28.

Conway, Jim. "Divorce and You." *HIS* (April 1979): 2.

Dobbins, Dr. Richard. "Don't Let Your Family Be a Statistic." *Charisma* (December 1979): 33.

Gundry, Patricia. "Submitting to Each Other in Marriage." *HIS* (June 1980): 22.

Marshall, Catherine. "The Coffeepot Experiment." *Guideposts* (February 1980): 6.

Nicholi II, Marmand M. "The Fractured Family: Following It Into the Future." *Christianity Today* (May 25, 1979): 11.

Sherrill, John. "The Husband of the Mother of the Bride." *Guideposts* (June 1980): 32.

"When My Parents Split Up." *HIS* (April 1979): 9.